Stones of Rimini

By the Same Author

★

THE QUATTRO CENTO

A DIFFERENT CONCEPTION
OF THE ITALIAN RENAISSANCE

STONES OF RIMINI

ADRIAN STOKES

SCHOCKEN BOOKS · NEW YORK

First published in Great Britain in 1934

First SCHOCKEN edition 1969

All rights reserved

Library of Congress Catalog Card No. 69–14801

Manufactured in the United States of America

For
MOLLIE HIGGINS
with love

this book in which so many ideas
are the fruit of her perception

Contents

PART ONE : *STONE AND WATER*

PART TWO : *STONE AND CLAY*

PART THREE : *STONE, WATER AND STARS*

Illustrations

NOTE. *Except where otherwise stated all the illustrations are from the Tempio Malatestiano (1447-61 approximately) at Rimini, and are of the sculpture of* Agostino di Duccio *or his assistants*

9

Illustrations

Illustrations

11

Part One

Stone and Water

Chapter One

Stone and Water

I write of stone. I write of Italy where stone is habitual. Every Venetian generation handles the Istrian stone of which Venice is made. Venetian sculpture proceeds now, not by chisel and hammer, but under the hands, the feet, under the very breath of each inhabitant and of a few cats, dogs and vermin. See the nobs upon the ponte della Paglia, how fine their polish, how constantly renewed is their hand-finish.

Hand-finish is the most vivid testimony of sculpture. People touch things according to their shape. A single shape is made magnificent by perennial touching. For the hand explores, all unconsciously to reveal, to magnify an existent form. Perfect sculpture needs your hand to communicate some pulse and warmth, to reveal subtleties unnoticed by the eye, needs your hand to enhance them. Used, carved stone, exposed to the weather, records on its concrete shape in spatial, immediate, simultaneous form, not only the winding passages of days and nights, the opening and shutting skies of warmth and wet, but also the sensitiveness, the vitality even, that each successive touching has communicated. This is not peculiar to Venice nor to Italy. Almost every-

15

where man has recorded his feelings in stone. To the designed shape of some piece, almost everywhere usage has sometimes added an aesthetic meaning that corresponds to no conscious aesthetic aim. But it is in Italy and other Mediterranean countries that we take real courage from such evidence of solid or objectified feelings, quite apart from the fact that these are the countries of marble, of well-heads and fountains, of assignation or lounging beneath arcades and porticoes, of huge stone palaces and massive cornices where pigeons tramp their red feet. We are prepared to enjoy stone in the south. For, as we come to the southern light of the Mediterranean, we enter regions of coherence and of settled forms. The piecemeal of our lives now offers some mass, the many heads of discontent are less devious in their looks. When we stand in the piazzas of southern towns, it is as if a band had struck up; for when grouped at home about our native bandstand we have noticed the feeble public park to attain a certain definiteness. Similarly we are prepared in the southern light to admire the evidence of Italian living concreted and objectified in stone.

But exhilaration gained from stone is a vastly different encouragement from the one that music may afford. It is an opposite encouragement. Or rather it is something more than the bestowal of a tempo on things. For tempo, the life-process itself, attains concreteness as stone. In Venice the world is stone. There, in stone, to which each changing light is gloss, the human process shines clear and quasi-permanent. There, the lives of generations have made exteriors, acceptable between sky and

16

water, marbles inhabited by emotion, feelings turned to marble.

Without a visit to Venice you may hardly envisage stone as so capable to hold firm the flux of feelings. Stone sculpture apart, stone is more often conceived in the north as simply rock-like. And who will love the homogeneous marble sheets in the halls of Lyons' Corner Houses? No hands will attempt to evoke from them a gradual life. For nowhere upon them is the human impress. Few hands have touched them, or an instrument held in the hand. They were sliced from their blocks by impervious machines. They have been shifted and hauled like so many girders. They are illumined in their hues beneath the light; yet they are adamant.

In writing now of Venice, I have not in mind Venetian sculpture nor marble palaces reflecting the waters between them. I refer to the less signal yet vast outlay there of the salt-white Istrian stone, every bit of it used; to bridge-banisters and fondamenta-posts made smooth and electric by swift or groping hands and by the sudden sprawls of children; to great lintels seared like eaten wood above storehouse doorways on the Giudecca; to the gleaming stanchion on the quay in front of the Salute, a stanchion whose squat cylindrical form is made all the more trenchant by the deep spiral groove carved by the repeated pull of ropes; to vaster stanchions on the Zattere, lying as long and white and muffled as polar bears. . . . Stone enshrines all usage and all fantasies. They are given height, width, and breadth, solidity. Life in Venice is outward, enshrined in gleaming white

Stone and Water

Istrian. Each shrine is actuality beneath the exploring hand, is steadfast to the eye. Such perpetuation, such instantaneous and solid showing of a long-gathered momentum, gives the courage to create in art as in life. For living is externalization, throwing an inner ferment outward into definite act and thought. Visual art is the clearest mirror of this aim. The painter's fantasies become material, become canvas and paint. Stone the solid, yet the habitat of soft light like the glow of flesh, is the material, so I shall maintain, that inspires all the visual arts. Marble statues of the gods are the gods themselves. For they are objects as if alive which enjoy complete outwardness.

In Venice, even pain has its god-like compass. Masks of toothache, masks of suffering, snow-white, incorrigible, overhanging dark waters, these great stone heads line the base of the palazzo Pesaro on the side canal. The gondolier who enters from the Grand Canal will need to use the masks to correct his black boat. He thus polishes one or two heads, damps the swollen cheek of another, strikes a hollow roaring mouth. The cries from canal and from calli, new noises that are caught to the clammy, still livid recesses of the stone, released old and thin and ominous as echo, are as sustenance to these perennial faces. . . .

That a stone face representing Vice or toothache should be an assistance in navigation, that misery should be exemplified as solid, attaining beauty in completeness, lends to all phenomena, even the least welcome, an almost positive zest. And see how these stones make permanent drama of the sky's shifting materials!

Stone and Water

Istrian marble blackens in the shade, is snow or salt-white where exposed to the sun. Light and shade are thus recorded, abstracted, intensified, solidified. Matter is dramatized in stone, huge stonework palaces rebutting the waters.

No: it is the sea that thus stands petrified, sharp and continuous till up near the sky. For this Istrian stone seems compact of salt's bright yet shaggy crystals. Air eats into it, the brightness remains. Amid the sea Venice is built from the essence of the sea. Over the Adriatic, mounted upon churches and palaces, a thousand statues posture, distilled agleam from the whirls and liquid tresses of the Adriatic over which they are presiding. They stand white against the sky, one with a banner, another with a broken column in her hands.

Yet this whiteness as of salt is not dazzling. On the contrary, though here the sea is petrified, it still is ruffled or is cut into successive cylinders and pillars. Istrian stone has always been hammered. It is a convention of its use which probably arose in the construction of bridges and water stairs. For this hammering, which makes the smallest surface a microcosm of the larger growths in light and shade, prevents the stone from being slippery. So, we are reminded of the substances that batten on slippery rocks and roughen them, shells with crusted grooves, or hard sponges. When such thoughts are uppermost, Istrian stone itself, Venice herself, is an incrustation.

Or again at night, Istrian is lace. The Baroque fronts are like giant fretworks that stiffen the brighter stars. Lace, in fact, has always been an industry in Venice, though more particularly at Chioggia where they have woven it large and coarse.

Again, if in fantasy the stones of Venice appear as the waves' petrification, then Venetian glass, compost of Venetian sand and water, expresses the taut curvature of the cold under-sea, the slow, oppressed yet brittle curves of dimly translucent water.

If we would understand a visual art, we ourselves must cherish some fantasy of the material that stimulated the artist, and ourselves feel some emotional reason why his imagination chose, when choice was not altogether impelled by practical, technical and social considerations, to employ one material rather than another. Poets alone are trustworthy interpreters. They alone possess the insight with which to re-create subjectively the unconscious fantasies that are general.

Agostino di Duccio's reliefs in the Tempio Malatestiano at Rimini (which provide the majority of the illustrations[1] in this book), so far as they reflect, and even concentrate, the common Mediterranean fantasies of stone and water, for their interpretation require an account of Mediterranean geography and the dependent scope of Mediterranean visual art seen as a whole.

An invocation of Venice has been my prologue. For the Venetian stones and waters are the Mediterranean essence: how strongly Mediterranean is this essence, you may judge from any port or harbour in the world. For, wherever it may be, the stone jetties and circumvented

[1] All the illustrations, except five, are from the Tempio.

Stone and Water

waters that make a port are reminders of the Mediterranean scene.

Even the port of London has its Mediterranean aspect, where at Wapping or Limehouse the stout warehouses are steeped in the river. The Genoa-like passages between them are narrow and tall: at their ends you emerge into the light and into the open, discover an array of steps, or a quay that locks the river in a seething stone or brick embrace. The stones retain an equal warmth if the sun is out, an equal radiance that contrasts with the polyp-like elongations and contractions of the water's glassiness.

The water never palls against the stone: the radiant causeway swarms. Water and builded stone vivify the one the other; they are at peace. The certainty of man-placed stones contracts the ocean's awfulness. In the port, it is as if the seas had been sifted and winnowed: upon the tall mole we can admit and gaze at their depth. Nothing is kinder to the ephemeral movements, the ephemeral reflections, refractions and shadows of water than the even-lighted masonry; no material less stalwart would provide such vivid opportunities to the water's reflective tricks.

Amid the hurly-burly of the port there exists the wideness of all space in miniature, the Mediterranean spaciousness or distinctness. In the harbour world of stone and water—this open, flat, world of different levels—there exist the broad angles which airs and winds caress, there exist the means of promenade, of conversation, of taking the evening leisurely: there are stanchions and rails and other significant shapes, stations for human attitude: there exists the scenery for gesture. Acoustic is plain in echo. Without mutual interruption, sounds glide to and fro like gulls. Bells from the towers of the upper town, or from a church reached by steps from the quay, plumb with their peals the harbour's breadth and depth.

However great its merchandise, the port is a haven, a repose, a measurer of passing things. The sun moves round, warming in turn those mammoth recording dials, the moles and quays, which the well-travelled waters lap. The scene is animated but steadfast. At night the waters are the dial. They show a shimmering rod or a hesitant patch of light. We can hardly discern the quays: we hear against them the home waters as they weigh us down carefully with the heavy finery of sleep.

What looks more apprehensive than the whiter stones before a storm, at the moment when the fall of livid ripplets against beach or mole is a distinct and almost shattering sound? This horizontal world of masonry and moving water is the ideal setting for the perpendicular rain and for the lightning. The storm passes, the dampened stones remain: even the waters are bemused and deaf to the wind. Ourselves along the wharves, perpendicular as the forest of masts upon the ships, appear intensely human: our houses stand up well above the port to which each alley leads.

Of such sort is the scenery of maritime commerce, the typical setting, we shall realize, of Mediterranean culture. For in the port we witness those elementary ab-

Stone and Water

stractions of visual experience which have always governed to a greater or lesser degree the Mediterranean conception of visual art. Here, in simplest form, are elements which provoke the aesthetic conception of space, here is the broad immovable masonry laid out on different levels, and betwixt these arms of stone, the moving waters. The smallest boat leaves a track on the water's face: even a thrown pebble makes enlarging circles. These liquid movements enhance a thousandfold the solid radiance of the masonry. We come to see its stones as waywardness, as rhythm and movement, absorbed and transformed into a face of static substance; we see masonry as solid space, as an outwardness which symbolizes the sum of expression. In the clarid Mediterranean light which brings the distance near, which makes of the panorama and of all that happens there a single object, this order of stone is particularly impressive. But everywhere the light upon dressed stone shows evenly and thus recalls, when dramatized by the presence of deep yet domestic waters, the vivid outwardness of the Mediterranean scene.

This book is concerned with the imaginative meanings that we attach to stone and water in relation, so far as an emphasis put upon those meanings is essential to the interpretation of Agostino's Tempio sculpture. By virtue of this approach we discover or re-discover Mediterranean art and life, the character of limestone, the differences between carving and modelling, ancient theories of the stars. Agostino's sculpture makes cognate subjects of these.

Stone and Water

They are never discursions. So far as this book has any aim wider than to interpret the Tempio reliefs, it is as a symptom of altered culture. Today, and not before, do we commence to emerge from the Stone Age: that is to say, for the first time on so vast a scale throughout Europe does hewn stone give place to plastic materials. An attitude to material, an attitude conceived in this book as being far more than the visual-aesthetic basis of Western civilization, can hardly survive long. The use in building of quarried stone must, we shall argue, increasingly diminish, and with it one nucleus of those dominant fantasies which have coloured the European perception of the visual world. In the work of men, manufacture, the process of fashioning or moulding, supersedes, wherever it is possible, the process of enhancing or carving material, the process that imitates those gradual natural forces that vivify and destroy Nature before our eyes. Hitherto there has always existed a ratio, full of cultural import, between carving and modelling, terms on which we thus bestow the widest application.

We emerge from the Stone Age: and perhaps the very perception of stone manifest in this book, rather than any argument adduced, proves this to be so. For what is dead or dying is more simply an object, and therefore easier to apprehend, than what is inextricably bound up with the very flow of life. Nothing in writing is easier than to raise the dead.

Stone and Water

A Note of Specific Introduction

Those readers who are unacquainted with *The Quattro Cento: A Different Conception of the Italian Renaissance*[1] are not at a disadvantage in their reading of the present volume, the second of the series. The only matter that needs to be explained again is the use throughout this series of the expression 'Quattro Cento'.[2] The reader is asked to bear in mind that 'Quattro Cento' art means 15th-century Italian art in which fantasies connected with material (always in the last resort, stone), are directly and emphatically expressed. My present aim does not require me to assert once more the full distinction that this term is meant to imply, the distinction between Quattro Cento art and other 15th-century Italian art, nor to recapitulate either the historical or aesthetic grounds on which it is based. The Tempio, a Quattro Cento building, is not, as in the previous volume, compared or contrasted with other contemporary buildings. I need, however, to preserve this label, if only in the interest of further volumes that are projected: and since the Tempio is a Quattro Cento building so-called, everything that follows should gradually re-create or reinforce this conception, Quattro Cento. The writer is a fool (no poet) who formulates a definition when his whole book is intended as such.

One other point. The present volume does not fulfil the promise made in *The Quattro Cento* to give a com-

1 Faber & Faber, 1932; Schocken Books, 1968.

[2] Quattrocento (*sic*) as one word is the Italian chronological expression to denote 15th century. *As in Volume I, for the sake of distinctness this purely chronological expression will never be employed.*

Stone and Water

plete account of the Tempio. Chapter V, entitled *The Tempio: first visit*, is a description of that building as a whole: but it is cursory. This book claims to interpret fully a single aspect of the Tempio art, the one that is, perhaps, most significant. Agostino's sculpture, the themes of stone, and of stone and water, demand a book to themselves. And so, in the present volume, there has not been embodied to any large extent my researches into the history of the Tempio's construction, of its artists and of its founder, Sigismondo Malatesta, tyrant of Rimini. Matteo de' Pasti, Pisanello, Sigismondo and Isotta, Alberti, will, I hope, appear again in a subsequent volume to whose compilation the *Sigismondo Cantos* of Ezra Pound have long inspired me.

Chapter Two

The Pleasures of Limestone : A Geological
Medley

Stone is the earth's crust. There is a condition in one's appreciation of sculpture when for deeper understanding one must look at the lands, at mountains and valleys. The scale is too little organized for any single appraisal: but one must feel the omniscience of sculptural process when rain strikes a crag or as the sea embraces rocks and leaves them wet, or when winds abrade them with sand: we must see what joints of the rock frosts and glaciers have revealed. The weathering of stone is omnipresent. Pavements, no less than pebbles, are polished and shifted. To this sculpture we owe the clean shape of hills and peaks, to this sculpture, and to the carving movements of plant and insect life, we owe the transition from rocks to sub-soil, from sub-soil to earths. Earth is decomposed rock. The 'stonyness' of stone is but one aspect of its impression. The senses, hardly less than the intellect, can be aware that all minerals, all elements, are contained and concreted in stones.

Even the most unyielding stones are not repulsive. There are few minerals that do not possess some indication of geometric, crystalline character. Stones chip or burst under the hammer, but each stone chips or bursts according to the rules of its kind. The geometry of fracture limits and defines the art of carving. Stone has grain. Building stones, no less than wood, ought to be seasoned. Sir Christopher Wren refused for St. Paul's any stone that had not been quarried and exposed to the atmosphere for three years.[1] As a rule, stones must be allowed to retain in a building the same angle of inclination that they enjoyed in their beds. Some stones smell strongly. Fetid limestone, when struck with a hammer, emits sulphuretted hydrogen. There is an Indian sandstone a slab of which can be bent.[2]

An ill-conceived blow, particularly with a blunt tool, can stun or bruise stone of whatever kind. It is likely that the bruised place will spall off sooner or later: for the particles have suffered a fracture of their cementing material. Meanwhile the place has probably lost its

[1] It is probable, however, that Wren's exposure of the blocks was not dictated so much by a conception of seasoning as by the desire to witness a general weathering that would enable the detection of any fundamental weaknesses. The actual seasoning of building stone is the formation on its surface of a hard crust from matter held in solution within the stone. On exposure, this matter is drawn by capillary attraction to the surface where its water is evaporated and the crust is formed. Thus, in varying degrees, all stones are softer when first quarried. Roman travertine is said to be so soft before seasoning that it can be cut with a spade. However, from the point of view of endurance, it is a much debated point whether the stone should be dressed before or after seasoning, that is to say, before or after the so-called quarry sap has formed a hard surface skin. (Cf. *The Weathering of Natural Building Stones*, R. J. Schaffer, Stationery Office, London, 1932, p. 16.)

[2] There is an example of this stone in acrobatic pose at the Geological Museum, another at the Natural History Museum, London.

A Geological Medley

colour; or perhaps it appears infected with ill-assorted spots.

Modern geologists show a tendency to withhold many of the millions of years that have hitherto been required for geological time. In some cases of sedimentary deposition, stone forms itself quickly enough. In Green Lake, New York State, for instance, algae are building fringing reefs of limestone. They deposit thick incrustation upon the branches and trunks of trees that have fallen into the water.[1] At the Kensington Natural History Museum one may see similar incrustations upon a human skull recovered from the Tiber. At Knaresborough, near Harrogate, there is a petrifying well. Its water contains a large amount of dissolved minerals that are deposited upon objects suspended where the water drips over them. In Auvergne springs[2] of similar powers, moulds of gutta-percha or sulphur taken from reliefs and cameos receive a limestone cast.[3] Travertine, the limestone with which Rome was built, is daily deposited as fur in kettles. The boiling of water precipitates, in the form of calcium carbonate or limestone, the bicarbonate of calcium that our water holds in solution. The North Bridge, Edinburgh, was finished in 1772. In 1882, stalactites, an inch and a half in diameter, depended from it.

All the above instances of mineral formation are of

[1] See *Algal Reefs and Oolites of the Green River Formation*, W. H. Bradley, U.S. Geological Survey, 1929.

[2] See *Proceedings of Geologists Association*, London, 1902.

[3] They should be employed to decorate our modern buildings of concrete or moulded stone. Hitherto man has dressed or carved stone which Nature had in the first place moulded. Now man can model the stone with which he builds. The bouleversement entailed in aesthetics is discussed at the end of the fourth chapter.

The Pleasures of Limestone

limestone, a sedimentary rock, as are sandstones and clay conglomerates as well. The sedimentary rocks are those commonly used in building: it is with them that we associate the weathered surfaces which enhance the meanings of stone described in the first chapter. Sedimentary structure, particularly the lie of the beds, gives character to masonry no less than to the cliff. In Ham Hill, Doulting, and in certain of the Bath stones, for instance, soft beds of clay alternate with the purer limestone, an alternation which, though sometimes the cause of weakness, since the clay tends to be washed thin, bestows on masonry a sculptural responsiveness. To this marked bedding of sedimentary rocks is due the ease with which they are handled: since they are inclined to have a laminated fracture in accordance with their beds, and so they are easy to thin. This fact is of immense importance for any consideration of the character of stone carving, so far as its procedure is best illustrated by the cutting of sedimentary rocks. Carving of all stones, we shall find, is essentially a thinning: all sculpture that reverences the stone manifests thinned or flattened forms. The sectional model for the process of carving is a shale bed: every piece of shale or slate possesses a pure laminated structure. Shale is the softer: we may see a bed cut by the sea to almost paper-like tiers of thinness, a flat or plated expanse revealed by the outlying tide, grateful to bare feet, yet possessing between each tier and its neighbour the tiniest and most smooth of precipices. Or we may pick up that perfect piece of sculpture rubbed by the sea, the flattened yet rounded slate whose smooth face can be thrown to skim and leap the waves.

A Geological Medley

The plated cleavage of slate, however, has no relation to the bedding of the original sediment which was clay. Slate is metamorphosed clay, that is, clay whose structure and substance has been altered by the effects of heat or pressure or of both. Soapstone, one of the softest stones, is also metamorphic rock constructed of thin scales or plates. Marble, a considerably harder rock, is metamorphosed limestone. The simplification of structure entailed in metamorphosis has largely determined sculptors' preference for metamorphic rocks, at any rate when their aim could be characterized as a naturalistic one: or perhaps it would be more true to say that the simplified structure (for thinning purposes) of some metamorphic rocks, particularly marble, has largely determined the aim and scope of naturalistic styles.

Marble, then, is metamorphosed limestone. Since marble shares with limestone all the qualities that concern us, I shall, especially in the next chapter, often use the one term 'limestone' to denote them together. In any case, my subject centres around the purer kinds of limestone which, in some varieties, Istrian stone for example, approximate closely to marble. But all limestones, to greater degree than the other sedimentary rocks, and to a yet greater degree than the igneous rocks, possess a substance that provokes from water, the dominant natural carving force, a most palpable sculpture. Calcium carbonate or calcite, the basic mineral of limestone and marble, is almost insoluble in pure water: but nearly all water, including the fresh rain, holds carbon dioxide, which has the power, in some degree, to dissolve calcium carbonate. The most fantastic as well as

The Pleasures of Limestone

the most peaceful scenery is of limestone. Caves and grottoes, it is true, may be cut in any stone. There are porphyry grottoes, even, near Quito in Ecuador. But as a rule, grottoes are limestone formations. Springs percolate limestone, rivers are fed by this rock. Under certain climatic conditions, limestone is the formation of workmanlike fertility in which agricultural interference not only is, but looks like, a work of art. Conversely, human agency can sometimes transform a wooded limestone district into a desert, and thus change the climate. Parts of Dalmatia are now a moon-like desert. The woods were cut down by Venetians to build ships, with the result that rainfall has decreased and temperature increased. Goats destroyed the young shoots: humus, deprived of trees, was washed through: the thirsty limestone was laid bare. Rain caused huge fissures and funnels, discharged itself into the subterranean streams and lakes of the present Karst country.

At one time or another deforestation has swiftly brought about similar conditions in many parts of the Mediterranean, particularly in Calabria and in Greece. It is this interaction between limestone and water, the spectacular responsiveness of limestone to the most palpable of Nature's carving tools, that provides us with a major theme. For the moon-like landscape is only one outcome of their interaction. Limestone that is also carved by vegetable life and by man, often provides the contours of a various and controlled plenty. It is the 'human' landscape which best shows man in accord with Nature. Limestone is the humanistic rock. The spectacular witness of limestone weathering or natural

A Geological Medley

sculpture has inspired many of the comprehensive images on which civilizations have been based, in those countries, at least, around the Mediterranean where the climatic condition to be described causes limestone to provoke images of the greatest power. The interaction of limestone and water is always poetic, always appealing to the imagination. In the first instance, it was the waters that fed those organisms whose remains formed the nucleus of limestones: it was the waters that carried the calcium carbonate which cemented those remains into rock. The story of limestone and water has many further chapters that are palpable to the senses, many variations: and the men who obtained nourishment from this environment soon conceived those many aspects of life and death which, when forming some calm or 'objective' whole, we name culture. Even directly, we shall deduce from the frequency of limestone in the Grecian and Italic lands, in the Mediterranean basin as a whole, fundamental fantasies that are readily projected as the fundamental forms [1] of classical visual art.

There is an association between man and limestone underlying all architecture. Most caves are in limestone. During unknown aeons caves were the homes of men. Limestone roofed them; upon limestone walls, as if upon the cognate plaster, they drew and incised figures. Some caverns, to our eyes, give the direct prototypes for particular architectural members. Columns of stalactite and stalagmite are an obvious example. These formations

[1] Whether these forms are of non-Mediterranean origin, or whether or not they are used independently in other parts of the world, does not immediately concern the argument.

The Pleasures of Limestone

are pure calcium carbonate deposited by the dripping of water. The Luray cavern in Virginia contains a fluted column of pure white marble of the finest grain, thirty feet high. There are natural corridors, galleries, amphitheatres of immense magnitude. One room has a dome supported by columns and walls of green and orange crystalline stone.[1] It is difficult to determine by sight the dimensions of cavernous rooms; for, since there are no particles floating in the air to scatter the rays of light, one is certain to exaggerate the magnitude of subterranean spaces. They loom, they suggest a Mohammedan or Gothic rather than a classical style. Still, one would imagine that when men came up to live in the sun, and when finally they realized the measure in outlook that one associates with the Mediterranean lands and the Mediterranean light, one would imagine that what remembrance remained of the looming cavern would be exorcized, translated into a broad and open architecture of precision; masonry placed on high in the sun, a single and clear organization of Nature's limestone bizarrerie. We shall find the Hellenic temple to be thus. Seen in the light, the detailed structure of limestone often displays classical members. For instance, at one point at least where horizontal strata are exposed on the cliffs at Lavenock, Glamorgan, one sees the delicate lines as architrave moulding and a projecting slab above as cornice.[2]

[1] See *Limestones and Marbles*, S. M. Burnham, Boston, 1883.

[2] Natural derivations are often suggested for architectural forms. When intended literally, inferring a conscious model, such suggestions are rarely opportune. But I see little harm in adding one more. It concerns the Ionic volute and the common limestone

A Geological Medley

Since those forces of Nature, particularly rain, of which we ourselves are continually aware, sculpture or weather limestone to effects more easily interpreted than in the case of other hard stones, the limestone scenery of a land tends to be its characteristic scenery. This stone puts climate outward for us as one thing. The usual features of hard limestone scenery are wall-like precipices, pinnacles and jagged peaks. These are common in limestones of the carboniferous period and also in dolomite, a limestone which contains magnesium carbonate. At the other extreme, to which Cotswold scenery, for example, of oolitic limestone, is intermediate, there are the soft rolling chalk downs of southern England. For chalk too is limestone. No other English scenery is considered to be so characteristic, and with reason. The downs suggest to us our climate in the solid. When we touch them we seem to hold our airs. Moreover, the down districts of Wiltshire and Sussex have probably undergone less change since the appearance of man than any other part of the country. For here are found neither glacial deposits nor extensive superficial weathering products. Rain soaks quickly to the chalk, leaves the turf springy. The higher regions have long been open pasture, and the lower ground arable. We must thank the chalk for the origin of our field games. Thus William Smith remarked, "The short turf on the Chalk Hills, the site of ancient British sports, the seats of

fossil known as an ammonite. This creature of concentric curves radiating from a heart reproduces in its petrified state the very logic of the volute's scroll-like structure, whereas the ram's horn, usually cited in this connection, resembles the Ionic volute only in the most general impression of its shape.

35

The Pleasures of Limestone

Druidism and ancient Kings, will ever continue to be favourite places of amusement: Gentlemen of the Turf having found this to be the best for ascertaining the comparative speed of British horses, the races of Newmarket, Epsom, Salisbury, Brighton, and several other places being on the stratum."[1]

The power of limestone, one formation among many, to bestow on lands the generalized image or character, is not to be explained without reference to its various aesthetic qualities, and to the decisive part limestone plays in water supply. As has been said, water is the weathering agency that grips the imagination, and the sculpting effects of water upon limestone are better apprehended than in the case of other stones. Granite or basalt cliffs are more resistant: they do not appear to have the same communion with the seas that make our soft chalk cliffs so clean and sheer, or that expose the joints and beds of so many carboniferous limestones and other calcareous rocks along our shores. As for the non-calcareous sedimentary rocks, clays, shales and sandstones, though they often display carven joints no less sculptural than those of some limestones, yet from the imaginative angle inspired by human need they do not equal limestone in their communion with water. For limestones, whether they are porous, or impermeable yet loose-jointed, are pre-eminently the rocks that allow water to accumulate in the earth. Limestone countenances the formation of springs and wells, of small-scale and well-distributed waters. And in temperate lands, at least, it is this question of the scale of water distribution

[1] *Strata identified by Organized Remains,* 1816.

36

A Geological Medley

that more than anything else determines the scale of the human vista. Limestone formation, especially when it is associated, as it generally is, with mountain-locked valleys and sudden ravines, encourages independent and small communities. The continental empires, on the other hand, radiate athwart the vastness of single rivers, their all-too-powerful fathers.

Only about a quarter of the rain that falls on the earth is reckoned to soak into the ground. Except for calcareous rocks this amount would be enormously reduced. The topography of giant rivers and the overpowering mythology to which they give rise would be almost universal: there would be far greater expanses of desert; and of morass, since clays and other formations of many but small pores soak in waters almost indefinitely without discharging them. From the human point of view, lime has a most beneficent effect on clay, causing the finest clay particles to coagulate and to form bigger particles that are better aerated and better drained.

Water soaks gradually through chalk. We have our English limestones, particularly the chalk, to thank for over four-sevenths of the total public water supply. It is true that limestones are distributed throughout the world,[1] but Europe possesses a good deal more than its share. Our plentiful limestone in Europe is one of the chief determinants of our wealth. Connected with the movement of water through limestone is the occurrence

[1] On account of their mode of origin, sedimentary rocks tend to be more widely distributed at the earth's surface than those of igneous origin. Underneath it is different. F. W. Clarke and H. S. Washington (*The Composition of the Earth's Crust*, U.S. Geological Survey, Professional Paper, 127) have estimated that the relative

The Pleasures of Limestone

in some limestone formations of valuable metallic ores that the water deposits. Iron, lead and zinc ores have been deposited in this way. Carboniferous limestone was the foundation upon which coal was laid down; and since iron is also found in these strata, the site of many iron and steel-making centres has been due to the presence of the three essential ingredients, iron ore, coal and limestone for flux. Lime, calcium oxide, is made by burning limestone. It is essential to the preparation of potash and soda, which are basic ingredients of many manufacturing processes. Lime—and this concerns us more directly—is also the basis of mortar, plaster and cement. Plaster has always been used as a dressing to limestone buildings, particularly to interiors. Its use was extended to brick and to every kind of building material. But, stylistically, it became in essence the adjunct of classical architecture, the limestone architecture *par excellence*.[1]

In 1927 in England, 33,000 tons of limestone were

abundance of the various classes of rocks in the outermost ten miles of the earth's crust, is as follows:

Igneous rocks - - - - -	95.00 per cent.
Argillaceous rocks (clays and shales) -	4.00 ,,
Arenaceous rocks (sandstones and conglomerates) - - - -	0.75 ,,
Calcareous rocks (limestones) - -	0.25 ,,

There are many types of limestone rock formation in active progress to-day.

[1] The Egyptians used lime-plaster or stucco. So did the Greeks. They sometimes mixed their plaster with milk and saffron to enhance the golden tint they valued so much in stone. For an account of the aesthetic importance of light on limestone, best seen on the white and golden varieties, cf. the concluding pages of this chapter.

A Geological Medley

used for glass-making.[1] Lime figures prominently in medical preparations: a list of the modern industrial uses of limestone would be extensive. My present concern, however, is better served by reference to that part of its imaginative appeal which found expression in Mediterranean art and which is not unconnected, I feel, with the agricultural uses of this rock. As is well known, lime is an essential ingredient in productive soils. Calcium carbonate is essential to the reproduction and growth of plants and animals. It has been reckoned that each cow takes per year at least one and a quarter hundredweights of lime from an acre of land to form milk: if the calves are reared, the lime of their skeletons also comes from the soil.[2] Calcium carbonate is present to some degree in many igneous, sandy and clayey soils. But often the amount is not sufficient, and 'liming' is necessary. Even soils composed of the decomposition of limestone may need to be 'limed', and need it more than other soils, if the calcium carbonate, which is easily separated from such soil, has been washed through by rains.[3] The interaction between lime and rain by which rain is conserved in the rock so often at the expense of lime in the soil, calls for the adjustment that man will make: so in the next chapter I shall have much to say about Mediterranean farming and its connection with the measured economy of Mediterranean civilization. Lime keeps soil neutral, prevents it from growing acid

[1] *Limestones*, by F. J. North, Murby, 1930, p. 420.

[2] Hunter, G. B., 'Lime: the basis of soil fertility', *Cement, Lime and Gravel*, 1929.

[3] Thus, impure limestones generally yield better soils than pure limestone.

or sour, and consequently infertile. It also prevents alkaline conditions and promotes oxidization of the organic material.

It is not necessary for my purpose to stress these chemical uses of limestone.[1] They do not contribute directly to aesthetic appeal nor do they carry any such insistence upon the imagination as do the many links between limestone and water. Yet it is not irrelevant to the attainment of a more intimate feeling for limestone as a building stone, and for the appreciation of certain styles of marble sculpture as we shall see, to realize in general the fruitful and life-giving nature of calcium carbonate. It is, however, far more relevant to know something about the genesis of limestone.

Limestone, for the most part formed of organic deposits, is the link between the organic and inorganic worlds.[2] Limestone exhibits in mummified state the life no longer found of the Silurian and other distant ages, just as the Istrian palaces of Venice present to us, in terms of space, the hoard of ancient Venetian enterprise. The very substance of limestone suggests concreted Time, suggests that purely spatial or objective world which limestone architecture has organized for

[1] If it were, I would have to be more careful in my partiality. Clay, for instance, is also an indispensable substance of direct and widespread use; in building too. From clay are made bricks, tiles and earthenware.

[2] Limestone formed by chemical precipitation, as in the case of the travertine and stalactites to which reference has been made, is comparatively rare. However, it seems now to be generally accepted that oolitic limestones, an extensive genus of limestone often used for building, particularly in this country, were formed by purely chemical precipitation.

A Geological Medley

us. Though they have lacked the knowledge of limestone's origin, yet the unconscious fantasies of many races have directed artists to attain spatial completeness in their use of this stone. Except in terms of these fantasies connected with limestone we cannot explain either the ebullient life, the stone-blossom of Quattro Cento marble carving, or the complete and final revelation, the spectacular translation of time into space implicit in Quattro Cento limestone architecture.

The forms of life that are concreted into limestone, though apparent enough in many structures and in fossils, were never understood as such. Yet by some part of the mind their history was apprehended, and thus served to inspire humanistic art. A deeper love of stone than any that obtained in other periods, alone will explain those basic aspects of the Renaissance that are here termed Quattro Cento. And what is true of the Quattro Cento is true in some degree of Mediterranean art as a whole. I do not mean to suggest, however, that these obscure feelings would have made themselves felt so strongly except that some limestones not only have direct aesthetic appeal but also practical advantages for building and sculptural purposes. As is usual in what concerns the imagination, different fantasies, connected with the same object, go hand in hand, enhance one another's power. Any great love has many roots, many perceptions.

So let us consider the genesis of limestone. Lime, in the first place, is set free by the decomposition of igneous rocks which make up 95 per cent of the earth's crust.[1]

[1] Cf. Clark and Washington, *op. cit.*

41

The Pleasures of Limestone

They contain on an average, it is reckoned, about 5 per cent of lime. This lime is carried in solution by rivers to the sea. Except under special circumstances it is not then deposited, since the amount of carbon dioxide in sea-water keeps the calcium carbonate in solution: it is, however, extracted from the water by animals and plants.[1] The deposits of their remains are cemented into limestone. Limestone is petrified organism. We may see hundreds of shell fossils on the surfaces of some blocks. Nor are the animal fossils rare. The skeletons of coral are common, so too of the crinoid, a kind of star-fish. These fossils were, and are, encountered continually in the quarries ; and however falsely ancient philosophy and science may have explained them, art, which employs in a more direct way deep unconscious ' knowledge', magnified the truth. Shells were a Quattro Cento symbol. They have a long history in classical architecture and sculpture. But it was the Quattro Cento carvers who in their exuberance contrived for them the import of momentous emblems. Marine decoration of every kind is abundant in Quattro Cento art: dolphins, sea-monsters, as well as the fruits of the earth and the children of men, encrust the stone or grow there. The metamorphosed structure of marble encouraged an extreme anthropomorphic interpretation of its original life. Needless to say, though marine symbols attained a heightened significance in the humanism expressed by Quattro Cento art, they are common to Roman and Greek art and to Mediterranean art as a whole. So we must contemplate

[1] There are fresh-water limestones of organic origin. But they are not common.

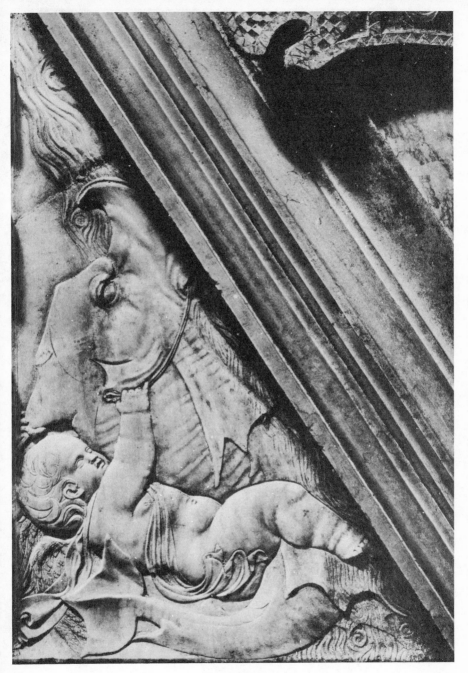

Plate 1. Putto on dolphin above tympanum of a door.

Plate 2. Angel holding up canopy on wall of first chapel to the right.

A Geological Medley

the entire Mediterranean basin in order to interpret the Quattro Cento achievement.

The sea and the limestone dominate those lands. The supply of fresh water springs from that stone. On our return from a visit to the South, we remember the limestone well-heads and the limestone fountains.

We begin readily to conceive the bond of classical building and limestone. No other architectural forms remind one so much of the horizontal bedding of stones. The jutting cornice, the architrave mouldings, the plinths and blocks, have a definite relation to the joints of stones as seen in quarry or cliff; and particularly to limestone, medium between the organic and the inorganic worlds.

A Greek temple is an ideal quarry reconstructed on the hill. The Tempio Malatestiano at Rimini is an ideal quarry whose original organic substances were renewed by the hand of the carver to express the abundant seas collected into solid stone.

Calcareous freestones and marbles have been the preferred stones used in building and sculpture throughout Europe. No other single factor has so widely determined the interrelation of styles, their limits and potentialities. Similarly, the scope of one kind of Egyptian carving can be deduced from the nature of granite. The aim of this book is to describe a building and its sculpture in which are employed the greatest love and feeling for limestone, and which, so far as the other visual arts admit stone-work as their parent, stands as the emblem of all European art.

43

The Pleasures of Limestone

The influence of material upon style is an aspect of art history that is never sufficiently studied, especially in relation to building. Before proceeding with limestone, let me consider this for a moment. You will not, for instance, find it remarked in books about English architecture that the fan vaulting in the cloisters of Gloucester Cathedral, the first vaulting of this kind in England and a departure full of consequence to English Gothic, was made possible, and perhaps largely suggested, by the use there of that extremely light stone, travertine. Again, the lightness of plentiful and local travertine explains many of the departures in Roman architecture, especially the Roman development of the arch. A few facts about their masonry will explain much of the inappositeness of so many modern stone buildings. Did there survive more than a lip-service feeling for stone, masonry would not be used at all when it is merely the screen to steel and concrete construction. But even apart from this use, our new metropolitan masonry would carry little conviction. When we visit an ancient stone building of no particular merit, we may yet find it of great interest so far as it makes us aware of its locality. For the building, if constructed of local materials, is an expression of its neighbourhood. We may even see upon the opposite hill a disused quarry from which the stones were taken. The building is part of the landscape carved by man: there exists the connection, though the building be an 18th-century palace, with the cave dwelling and the rock tomb. (For a fine house is not only a moulded thing but also a carved thing.) The stone may have come twenty, thirty miles;

no matter, it is better than three hundred miles. And this consideration is supported by a proverbial saying of quarrymen which scientists have failed to discount altogether: masonry weathers best in a building near the quarry. Though a block be taken to a region of identical climate, yet it weathers far better within a twenty-mile radius of the home quarry.

I do not suggest that there is, in itself, anything modern about the use of non-local stones for building. At all times choice stones have travelled to the sites of important buildings; and even inferior stones to regions which possess no rocks that supply masonry. It is a matter of degree, and of a consequent degree in change of attitude. Before transport became so easy, local stone usages were in far greater evidence: the respect for stone as a material of a particular character was widespread, strengthening the background before which national, and even international, architects worked. There was less of the modern moulding attitude to architectural design, and vastly more tradition in the employment of each kind of stone. Many million jerry-built, or semi-jerry-built, dwellings do not tend to heighten the non-plastic architectural sense. These dwellings are moulded like cheap tea-cups: the use of brick ceases to be any kind of substitute for stone. And if this has always been true to some extent of town architecture, it is a hundred times more true in the hey-day of science and machinery.

The barren plastic extreme in architecture was attained already in the eighteen-thirties when Royal Commissioners were hard at work looking for a suitable

stone with which to build the Houses of Parliament.
The designs of Barry and Pugin existed. It was the business of the Commissioners to find a stone which would
withstand the London atmosphere but which would, at
the same time, be soft enough to allow the easy execution of intricate and endless neo-Gothic ornamentation.
The Commissioners' task was an impossible one; since
the cart was not only before the horse, but of its nature
immovable. It may be recalled that an offer to supply,
free of charge, sufficient granite to build the Houses of
Parliament, had to be rejected owing to the difficulty of
working the stone to the accepted design. The Commissioners, buoyed up by cheap transport and modern
'science', encouraged by the sight in London of thousands of miles of insensitive paved streets, shouldered
their hopeless task. They took immense trouble to as-
certain the qualities of various stones: still, at bottom,
from the very circumstance of their task, they were re-
garding stone as modelling clay, just as do our contemporary architects who yet like to build with natural
stone. After finding that the Bolsover quarries would not
yield enough stone for their needs, the Commissioners
finally chose the lovely dolomite from Anston, an excellent building stone, but one which reacts to neo-Gothic
sculpture in London with dangerous vents and fissures.
The Geological Museum in Jermyn Street was built of
Anston stone at about the same time; and it is often
stated, with a certain amount of relish, that its good
condition is to be attributed to the personal choice of
the blocks made by Sir Henry de la Beche, who was
director at that time of H.M. Geological Survey. This is

A Geological Medley

probably entirely beside the point. There are vents in the ashlar wall: but they are of no consequence. The difference of design is explanation enough of the difference in condition.

There is no need to pursue the subject beyond this point of mere indication as to how plastic were the excesses of neo-Gothic (and therefore how grotesquely different from the Gothic which was aped in the most insensitive and stupid fashion), and how inevitable (historically), and how relieving, it is that the better contemporary architects who now command a wealth of purely plastic materials should desire to oust stone architecture altogether. Let us leave this digression with the thought that Athens was mostly built of the local Pentelic marble, Rome of the neighbouring travertine from Tivoli, while London's native building stone, Kentish Rag, is no more than a moderate kind of sandy limestone. That fine limestone, Portland stone, has well served London where it has been employed for hundreds of years. But London has never become a province of Dorset, as Venice became an offshoot of Istria.

There is a contemporary consciousness of the decay of building stones, due to its great increase and to the expense it involves. For the modern increase of decay we have to thank the modern plasticity in the use of this, and other, materials. Such indifference is often aggravated in its effects by the curative procedures[1] of a mercenary science. Again, machine dressing is sometimes

[1] Cf. the immense harm done to masonry by the association of alkalies in quick and cheap steam-cleaning processes. Schaffer, *op. cit.*, p. 94.

stated to bruise the stone no less than a blunt chisel. But infinitely greater destructive powers are at work, such as the soot and acids contained in urban atmosphere, and cement mortar jointings so strong or so dense as to impregnate both stone and brick with soluble salts. Exfoliation, florescence, the dreaded crypto-florescence (an internal wall-white or wall-cancer) and other diseases, are the outcome.

In truth, all stone weathering is stone disease. No stone resists the action of atmospheric agencies indefinitely: otherwise we would have no sediments, no soil, no natural sculpture. Chemical change belongs to the beauty and liveliness of stone: it is the natural carving that records Time in immediate form with the pattern and colour of surface. Only a few of these effects, therefore, are repulsive, exfoliation in particular, especially when it appears to be the result of a bacterial infection. As for durability, fine building stones that have been well treated and that are washed by the rains last long enough, even in the sulphurous air of London.

Of all weathering, that of limestone, as a rule, is the most vivid. It is limestone that combines with gases in the air, that is carved by the very breath we breathe out. It is limestone that forms new skins and poetic efflorescence: above all, limestone is sensitive to the most apparent of sculptural agencies, the rain. None the less, the exposed limestone that is well watered may escape harmful sulphate crusts; and such calcium carbonate as is removed by water may well be deposited elsewhere on the building, not in sufficient quantities as to be grotesque or dangerous, but enough to intimate the sculptural communion between the masonry and the water piercing and renewing its stones. It is partly this weathering effect in particular that causes limestones to be the most attractive of building materials. Clayey stones are not good for building, and their light is often dull; while the weathering of sandstones is often an unrelieved crumbling away, if, as is usually the case, the cementing materials between the grains are more sensitive than the grains themselves. A slight crumbling of the cement entails the flaking of what might seem disproportionately large pieces from a rock otherwise so hard. Or else, sandstones of a hard, siliceous, cement approximate in character to the abrupt and impervious granite which may become friable before the assaults of frost and other thermal changes, or, in the sea, before the activities of the rock-boring clam; but which seems to lack any communion with the elements that is continuous. It is not often that we see granite in the sensitive state of Cleopatra's needle, responsive after thousands of years of Egypt to the untoward atmosphere of London.

Even granite is heightened by human touch. Continual contact with hands and clothes causes nearly all stones to develop a smooth surface which is seldom observed to flake off. Examples of such surface are to be seen on those parts of ancient buildings that are accessible to the sculpture of touch. But, naturally, nowhere is this effect more palpable than in Venice, particularly on the banisters of the bridges, as we have observed.

Generally, however, natural sculpture would seem to militate against the durability of stone. The weathering of limestone may be beautiful; but is limestone a strong and lasting building stone? It is: at least many of the finer stones are most durable.[1] Fine structure and porosity, like a fine body, can attain a beautiful adjustment, can withstand the worse ravages of the many diseases to which all limestones are heirs. Whereas this is not true of the calcareous element in some dolomites and sandstones, the compactness of granular structure, the paucity of the cement, in the purer limestones, make them exceedingly robust stones. Of great importance are their capillary powers to draw soluble salts and other damaging moistures on to the surface. Stones with large pores put the ingredients of their chemical crystallizations outward. The size of the pores rather than their number is the point; and it is probably the greater size of the pores of Whitbed Portland that makes it a better building stone for outdoor use than the Basebed Portland.

The limestones and marbles of which Greek temples were built are today in fair condition, such as remain

[1] Another important point in favour of limestone is that it can be healthily worked. The chipping of siliceous stones, on the other hand, such as clays and most sandstones in particular, tends to be unhealthy. Tuberculosis and silicosis, for instance, are often directly traced to this source. Silica, to some degree, is present in all rocks except the majority of limestones. What influence, if any, this fact has had in determining the preference that limestone has enjoyed for building and carving, it is impossible to estimate. Perhaps the extent of silica in the rock to hand has partly confined the extent to which some cultures have depended upon stone architecture and sculpture for their expression. At any rate, we know that in Europe, whose extensive visual arts have so largely been bound up, directly and indirectly, with the working of stone, limestone is abundant, and has been employed to an infinitely greater extent than any other stone.

after rapine and earthquake. The vastly older Pyramids were built chiefly of Nummulitic[1] limestone. The quantity employed was enormous. "The Great Pyramid alone contains sufficient stone for the erection of 10,000 dwelling houses each of 8000 cubic feet capacity and with walls one foot in thickness."[2]

Rain, we have said, does not, as a rule, wash the weathered limestone appreciably away; yet it sculptures it more than other stone. One is aware of an intimacy in the *contact* between the marble fountain, for instance, and its water which here produces a gleaming surface veined with unsuspected colours, here magnifies fossil or granular structure. It is a matter of degree (for all stone is influenced by water), the degree of intimacy in their connection; and we have seen that the connections between limestone and water are diverse and poetic. One need know nothing about stones to distinguish a limestone fountain from one of granite. The sense of saturation they convey is different.[3] The granite fountain seems impervious, the water glassy: the limestone or marble fountain, on the other hand, seems to become organic beneath the water, to be sluiced, refreshed. It is not impervious, though solid and gleaming. The

[1] A limestone deposited by the fauna of the genus Nummulites, so called from its resemblance to a disc or coin (Latin: *nummarius*, pertaining to money). Strabo, referring to the disc forms visible on the Pyramid blocks, says that they (the discs) were supposed to be the petrified remains of food (lentils) eaten by the Pyramid builders as they worked.

[2] *Limestones, op. cit.*, p. 367.

[3] Contrast, for instance, the basin of the fountains' frontage in Kensington Gardens (Portland stone) with the granite fountains in Trafalgar Square.

The Pleasures of Limestone

water is the finery of a caressing mother. There is re-enacted the strong, resistant, coagulation of stone birth. A wet statue on a limestone fountain truly bathes. For purer limestones and marbles have an inner glow that disarms petrifaction of deathliness, though there is retained all the outwardness and objectivity of death. We sense a double petrifaction of this kind, the one in the making of the stone, the other in the making of the statue. Such quality, in combination with the comparative facility with which limestone can be cut, lends itself to the particular naturalism which we identify with Europe. Its origin, of course, and the scenes of its triumph, have been along the Mediterranean basin where marble and pure limestone abound, and where the geography is the limestone geography *par excellence.*

The compactness of their grains causes the purer limestones to be not only robust as we have seen, but also to possess in many cases this flesh-like glow. The radiance or glow of the purer limestones and marbles causes them, in combination with the impressive fact of their solidity, to be the symbols of life concreted into static objects, of Time concreted as Space.

The purer the limestone, the lighter its colour. The finest limestones are white, cream or golden; but even the whitest have some golden light. For the sake of the reader who can identify a few common building stones, but who does not realize as yet that they are limestones, I shall enumerate some of the light-coloured oolitic building stones of our own country. First, there is the

A Geological Medley

Portland stone from Dorset, well-known to Londoners,[1] then Bath stone, Ancaster, Ham Hill, Doulting, Dundry, Hayder, Weldon and such Cotswold stones as the one from Nailsworth, and the one from Painswick which closely resembles the Caen stone of Normandy extensively used in Paris. These are all light-coloured limestones of the same geological period. There are in England many other limestones of the same period, and, of course, limestones of other periods. If the reader can identify one name of the above list, the ensuing analysis of light on limestone will be more real to him. Fairly pure limestone only, and marbles, concern us. The proportion of siliceous (quartz or clay) minerals in so-called limestones is sometimes large. Kentish rag, for instance, is a limestone, but in many cases a very sandy, crumbly one. So is the beautiful Whitby stone.

Limestone's glow is not the result of transparency but of slight translucency or luminosity. Marble, more compact than limestone, is, on occasion, slightly transparent. Yet neither the comparative opaqueness of limestone, nor the reflective polish and transparency of dressed marble, overpower the other quality they have in common, the glow that is the opposite of the hard or glassy light of granite. Such soft and, in whitish stones, slightly roseate, radiance, evenly distributed, is due, we have said, to a fine granular structure that rocks which are conglomerates of the harder quartz in particular,

[1] Most of the City churches, including St. Paul's, are faced with Portland stone. Somerset House is another example. Portland stone was first used in London by Inigo Jones for the Banqueting Hall in Whitehall and other buildings. Cf. *The Stones of London*, J. V. Elsden and J. H. Howe, Colliery Guardian Co., 1923.

such as granites and sandstones, do not possess to the same degree. Although light penetrates most limestones readily, it becomes scattered and diffused in passing from one grain to another. All dressed stones are characterized by their diffused or equal light, but limestones especially. The light does not go straight through them as through a piece of calcite, but rather, it illuminates somewhat the interior, thus causing the otherwise opaque rock to have a certain quality of glow. As a rule, sandstone is more porous: light does not penetrate far. The sandstone's distinguishing light-effect is a glitter more or less, to which each surface grain contributes. The granular structure of a rock largely determines its appearance. Two transparent and equally polished spheres of the same size, the one calcite, the other quartz, cannot be distinguished by the eye: compacted into stone, however, their difference is obvious.

Granite is glassy in its light, without radiance, inhuman: and what is true of granite is true, to some extent, of all igneous rocks. Their basic element is silicon. The abundance and complexity of silicon compounds in the inorganic world is analogous to the vast number of complex carbon compounds in the organic world. Calcium carbonate, however, is a carbon compound. Once again we find limestone as a bridge between the organic and inorganic spheres.

Granite is composed of quartz, felspar and mica, all of them silicates. Felspar is only a little less hard than quartz. Mica is softer: but since it has an easy scale-like cleavage, similar in this respect to slate, a cleavage of thinning that is infinite, mica retains a more or less unaltered facet. Everyone has seen grains of mica glittering in pavements. Mica is inextinguishable, with no more radiance than quartz. We see the mica constantly in sandstones and granites. Felspar is opaque. So the light that passes through the mica and the quartz on the surface of granite is reflected straight back by the opaque felspar. In sandstones, the cement between and behind the grains often has this role. Once more, the comparative luminosity of so many limestones is due to the closeness of their grains. This luminosity, let me repeat, is not to be confused with transparency. Alabaster has a far more pronounced inner light; but alabaster, to a greater extent than marble, is transparent: so, the identification between an opaque or bluff appearance and a slight roseate glow is less marked in alabastrine and many semi-precious stones whose clean-cut qualities are those of gems rather than of building and sculptural blocks.

So much in explanation of the light of purer limestone, a diffused glow the opposite to glitter, to metallic high spots, to light-and-shade effects. It is a uniform[1] radiance, flesh-like and complete. It is the medium of that one-piece or spatial outwardness which is yet the sum of vitality. The work of a few great architects and sculptors reveals this to us. Thus, for my own part, it has been the Quattro Cento artists who have excited in me

[1] It is my belief that the tones of limestone underlie much painting, particularly the tonal painting of the Renaissance. This subject belongs to a later volume. Nor can I now argue the presumption I have made throughout this chapter that the working of stone has influenced the character of all the European visual arts. Both these subjects, however, particularly that of stone architecture as the parent art, were more than touched upon in *The Quattro Cento*.

The Pleasures of Limestone

so much love and so much interest in limestone. Now therefore, for the sake of one of them, Agostino di Duccio by name, I discuss limestone and the Mediterranean.

I have defined but cursorily the distinction between limestone and marble; since what I have needed to say was largely applicable to both. A polished white marble certainly glitters, but only as a lump of sugar glitters. The diffusion of some light remains, in some cases is even thus enhanced; because however intense the polish, partly because of it, one is conscious of uniform scattered light within the stone, as if it were the air which the stone breathed. Marble *is* limestone, re-crystallized limestone, limestone that as a result of heat or pressure has suffered re-crystallization, often at the expense of its original structure.[1] Pure marble is almost white. Other bright colours in marble are generally due to the presence of metallic compounds; while black marble is the result of decaying vegetation enclosed in the original limestone.[2]

From the aesthetic angle, the higher luminosity of marble is offset by its lack of perceptible structure, apart from what colour patterns it may contain. This lack of structure, however, in the case of the pure or statuary marbles at any rate, fits it further for carving; since the

[1] The stone trade tends to use the term 'marble' for any 'ornamental' stone, i.e., any stone that will accept polish. Such silicates as serpentine and porphyry, and an oxide such as onyx, are habitually catalogued as marbles. In the same way, hard sandstones and hard limestones are sometimes put on the market as 'granites'. Needless to add, such is not the usage in this book.

[2] If the rock cracked in the process of its change, the marble will have veins: if smashed and re-cemented, it will be a brecciated marble.

fracture, unlike that of quartz or flint particularly,[1] is regular. This advantage, added to its medium hardness, and added to the 'breathing' quality of its light, has been, I am convinced, a chief determinant of naturalistic styles. Moreover, in the hands of Quattro Cento artists, the loss of the link with its organic structure and origin allowed the sculptor greater freedom to re-create from such coherent mass, precise, imaginative and humanistic forms of sea-life and land-life.

The qualities of light here estimated are not, of course, nearly so apparent in dark or irregularly coloured limestone and marbles. It is perhaps significant that, although there are districts of calcareous rocks and of marble beds in China, they do not yield building stones of the kind I have praised,[2] the kind of which the Poros stone, common throughout Greece, white or golden of hue, is the model. The Japanese limestones are similar in this respect to the Chinese, although the Negato province produces a statuary marble, white Negato. It is, however, little used for sculpture. Granite seems to have been the only stone much employed for building in China and Japan, and then in small quantities.[3]

[1] Flint is a compact form of silica. The fracture of both flint and quartz is known as conchoidal, which means that it is deep at the centre of the fracture and sharp or shallow at the sides.

[2] Thus the Chinese oolitic limestones, that is, limestones of the same period as the light-coloured English stones listed above, are exceedingly dark of colour. Many other Chinese limestones are grey. No cretaceous strata have been found in Asia north of Tibet, east of the Urals, south of northern Siberia. Nor, in China, are there Tertiary deposits. White marble, such as was used to make the beautiful garden bridges of Pekin, is rare. See *Research in China*, Carnegie Institute, 1907.

[3] The famous exception is the Great Wall of China.

The Pleasures of Limestone

Probably 99 per cent of the buildings in Japan are composed of wood and paper.

If, from the angle of their visual arts, we call the European countries calcareous countries, then China and Japan are siliceous countries. For, the two substances we feel to be most representative of far-eastern art, clay and jadeite, are both silicates. Limestone is between the hardness of jade and the softness of clay. This intermediate substance is the mean of European art. It demands neither to be moulded like the clay, nor minutely whittled like the jade; but to be boldly carved.

Chapter Three

The Mediterranean

Each ancestry, each heritage attained outwardness in the compelling light of Mediterranean shores. That alone is the Mediterranean compulsion. No place is provincial, each place is self-contained. A continental climate, on the other hand, is a crude, browbeating force which moulds the men who come into it as if they had no ancestry: whereas the Mediterranean climate brings out their shape like the carver who externalizes the inner life of the stone. It is the difference between the uniform handling of a plastic process and the love for individual material exerted in a carving process. While the Russian of Kazan or Archangel can talk readily with the citizens of Moscow or Petrograd, neighbouring villagers in Italy often speak entirely different dialects. Other circumstances being equal, a continental climate will exact, in the end, an almost identical response from what were once the most diverse people.

One must realize that the majority of land is continental; one must realize that countries stretch and stretch. Whither do their mountains beckon, what animals, what races eat the plain, what things lie over their

The Mediterranean

vaster seas? One must realize that a continental sameness, a hardened rotation, a salient pursuit of day upon day, and year upon year, outdistances impressions of variegated and extemporary Nature, brings wholesale famine or wholesale plenty of one kind, enforces or obscures the simple and immense structure of which human life is a fragment and under which it is subsumed. Man is part of the landscape—Chinese paintings show him thus—and his animals and the animals which are not his are likely transmigrations of his aspect.

There is an opposite geography. The complete opposition is not between tropical or extreme climates and temperate zones, nor between a huge interior configuration and an island small or large. The opposite geography exists where man is master of the landscape, his background. Life on these most temperate coasts is still hard and fearful, but the air has clearness in which things stand.

Situation is fixed. No more will we speculate on the direction or tendencies of mountain or sea. We have arrived. These shores were the piazza of ancient life. It is still from here that we start to explore the hinterland. We northern Europeans still find that our first heritage, the first point of orientation, has been some part of the Mediterranean, Greece, Italy, and Judea. The grape, the olive, and the fig are yet the symbol of man's common need. Jehovah still walks his garden of myrtle, laurel, arbutus, cistus, juniper, evergreen-oak and wild olive, follows conduit paths in the cool of the evening.

It is a climate that shapes each varied fantasy: it is a variable relief that only repays the most diverse modes

60

of ingenious labour, it is a sea that washes tall and situated stones. On a blue day, the panorama from the summit of Mount Etna in Sicily has a radius of 130 miles. Mount Athos was a guide to seamen in the north Aegean for a radius of 100 miles. At the summer solstice its shadow falls on the market place of Myrina in the island of Lemnos forty miles away. Forty miles is the furthest distance from land in the Aegean.[1]

Cuneiform records from southern Mesopotamia refer to the Mediterranean as the 'sunset sea'. For the Mediterranean lay to the west of King Sargon and those dynasties. Still, such a description, however natural, to some part of our mind seems alien. For, northern though we are, the Mediterranean is not the southern sea to our fantasy: it is something far more original, something we have put in opposition to all seas and oceans outlandish. Away from the Mediterranean countries stretch. I for one expect even a Japanese to feel in Greece or Italy that here is the home of man. In the Mediterranean basin three continents meet; here they are resolved, it is here they have their fronts between the blue of sky and sea, here are the children of their intercourse, the Sporades, the Cyclades, Cyprus, Crete, Lampedusa, Naxos and the Balearic isles, all different, all approximate; for all partake of that distinct and static region betwixt the far-hurled, lush, the brutal North, and swarming deserts to the south and east.

The Mediterranean light and light-change is so real,

[1] These and other facts in this chapter are mostly drawn from Miss Semple's admirable *The Geography of the Mediterranean Region* (Constable, 1932), for which I express gratitude.

the day so broad. Thus, it is the suggestion of dream state, implicit in the phrase the 'sunset sea', that comes as a shock when connected with the Mediterranean. But mankind has always envisaged in the fiery yet liquid solution of the sunset, some state that is marshalled like the universal death, a celestial life in further western air. It is the plea for immortality beyond the illumined wrack where the sun goes to sea, a life within a liquid and diaphanous sun propped out of sight by waves. We can look at the sun at its going, and thither we are drawn in fantasy, forsaking the eastern dark for some low, nocturnal day lit by occidental beams to which the wandering sun returns for plenitude. The Greeks, too, created myths from such emotion, but neither the sun nor any other elemental power had the exorbitance in that climate to submerge their poetry with over-compulsive longing. Theirs was the full life, theirs the life-giving poetry for which each element of Nature was loved for its seemingly wayward and *informal* behests. Man will make of them formal gods, statues for the sea and for the rain, and even for the momentary lightning, eyeless statues of human stature. As sculpture are the lands, as sculpture the mountains and their vales, as sculpture the promontories and the tesselated seas.

And when Plato again set his thoughts upon the west, upon Atlantis, he was questioning the whole egocentric position on which Greeks and Romans in particular constructed Mediterranean culture. In the Renaissance, that culture attained its potent affirmation: its final affirmation; for already men were moving further west: soon America, soon Copernicus and his theories by

which the astronomical foundation of egocentric feeling
was destroyed, leading away from grandiose fantasies
based upon the senses, leading on to pure science and
the industrial age. Science has tracked the western sun:
it is true that it does not set. But what Atlantis is this
that we have found?

I cannot answer. So for the time, that we may the
better understand the change, I ask you to draw nearer
to the Mediterranean scene. One must learn geography
in order to interpret an art and to re-create it in words.
I want to show how a Greek temple grew from its sur-
roundings, and, finally, how Agostino's reliefs in the
Tempio translate the composite fervour that the whole
Mediterranean basin inspires.

In the words of Miss Semple,[1] the Mediterranean region is in the main a climatic unit. "It has an outstanding type of climate of which the essential feature is the
seasonal distribution of the rainfall. This type is not confined to the Mediterranean region of Europe. It recurs,
on the west side of the continents, at about the same latitude, both in the northern and southern hemispheres,
in California, Middle Chile, the west side of Cape
Colony and South-west Australia. All these districts
have their Mediterranean climate restricted to a narrow
coastal strip too limited in area to attain historical significance. . . . Compared with other Mediterranean climatic regions, the Mediterranean combines the advantage of large area with a whole complex of other geo-
graphical advantages, with varied relief, location on an

[1] *Op. cit.*

63

The Mediterranean

enclosed sea, command of a long indented coast-line, access to three contrasted continents, proximity to land routes and marine routes, all contributing to the stimulating environment which left its mark upon ancient Mediterranean civilization; for advancing civilization was chiefly progressive adjustment to this environment by the people living within reach of the Mediterranean coasts."

The Mediterranean is the explored sea. Homer sings 'the clear-seen islands'. Navigation, it is true, was mostly restricted to the summer months, and the then prevailing Etesian winds caused great difficulty and danger: in a word, navigation was navigation, an art. It is the same with the soil. Mediterranean conditions are always the conditions that most suggest the need for the artist. Upon this sea and land the creations of men look natural, acceptable to the play of Nature. Such was the ratio, then, between man and Nature. Many other climates are more bountiful, many seas are more subdued, but somewhat at the expense of this ratio.

Horticulture stands to agriculture as the so-called Fine Arts stand to the handicrafts. Where gardens are native, one feels that man rejoices in his male power to cause Nature to fructify. Hot-house forcing, on the other hand, or oasis cultivation, approaches manufacture rather than art. Then Nature is not so much the paramour of man as some deadened process that can be worked with strict uses of water and heat. There is lost the intensity of coaxing.

It is the garden of semi-arid climates that suggests the sweetest harmony, that suggests to us the original garden; where trees blossom all the year round, where dark evergreens turn the long summer dusts to shapely and lighted and resplendent repose, where conduits decide the paths and alleys, where the proof of man's intercourse with Nature is some man-made shape, some sculpture, some flowering tub of terebinth, some marble for the water, and sudden statues in the thickets or amid the clearing of a grove.

The Mediterranean garden is essentially small-scale. The constituent features can be reduced to the smallest size, yet give their reassurance; so powerful is the ratio between god and man. Nature, in all these aspects of her intercourse with man, becomes a city of fashioned, human, gods that resemble the statues populating glades.

Gardens are native to Japan, to the Hawaiian islands, to Persia, Babylon, Egypt and Kashmir. But all of these, one suspects, lack the perfection of this ratio and the setting of clear light and clear shadow which makes the world most concrete, and man most creative. Just as Venice is no gesture, no extravagance, but a miraculous condition of Nature that *demands* art from man, art in its most dramatic, most wish-fulfilling forms, so thus in general the conditions of Mediterranean agriculture are nearly always gratifying to the aesthetic sense. Here produce so often demands the sculptural, domestic and architectural aid of man. The vine flourishes on trellis, the wine made from its fruit is drunk beneath its shade. Mediterranean orchards with the vines swung between the trees like festoons are already gardens. Olives love their man-made terraces that go in stone perspective up the piedmont. There are high walls

The Mediterranean

for the fruit-bearing trees, craterous stone structures for the preservation of water, the terracing of hills for the straight trees and for the gnarled and filagree olives. Everywhere there is the same ratio between art and growth that one finds in the garden, between the mineral and the vegetable, between tub and shrub, between sculpture and horticulture, between the statue and its wood.

Into this ratio are brought the characteristics of many climates that adjoin the Mediterranean. The general climatic position of the basin is a semi-arid one between the rainy north and the Sahara arid belt: and it is this reduction of three continents to a much diversified measure that gives the Mediterranean climate the universal appeal, the prolific ratio between god and man which I would deny to soft oceanic isles, to Kashmir or to continental Persia.

The classic art of Athens was the art of Attica, a region prodigious alone in olive, grape and limestone. These products furnished a civilization. Measure and beauty lay in the conditions of their use. Shapeliness was evoked from this thin soil and from this sea in the clear Mediterranean light. Such intense shape of meagre but essential things, just as the sight of the intensive Mediterranean cultivation, often wearies the visitor from the North. He hates to find every hill-side carved into terraces by man, he hates to see Nature so matter-of-fact, so loving beneath the peasant yoke. He finds so phantomless a lyric to be barren, just as he finds the Mediterranean formal garden to be without charm. Ah, but he cannot believe in Nature's certainty, clearness, decision. He has the habit to expect clouds and veils and enshrouding atmospheres which oblige the hesitant northern days. He cannot believe Nature bountiful unless she be somewhat remote or, at the other extreme, exotic. Her shapes are not unqualified in the North. She is the Virgin there, she is contaminated by man rather than fulfilled by him. That which he cajoles the landscape gardener seeks to hide with bluffing spinneys and irregular avenues. The northerner avoids the full fruits of any intercourse.

The outcome of Mediterranean life is shapeliness. Man's first intercourse with the sea was the quest therein of a most definite shape in clear waters, the fish. Driven out from the forests, conquered peoples have become fishermen. Fishing, amid the friendly inlets of a limestone relief, leads on to commerce. The tunny, whose food value is enormous, regularly came down to the Aegean from the Black sea. The early Mediterranean traders undertook long voyages to the tunny beds.

Owing to the equality of its light, the curves of carved or weathered limestone express great roundness, the more so when the piece is flattened but yet conveys roundness. Similarly, the shape of most fish affords one a deep sensation of roundness, since it is a flattened or gradual yet rounded shape. The needs of commerce, and the identity between fundamental land and sea shapes, stimulated one another. The great commercial and colonizing cities of Athens, Corinth and Megara were situated amid limestone strata, in lands which were unsuitable for grain and which intensified the necessity for commerce. Earlier Homeric cities, on the other hand, Argos, Mycenae and Tiryns, were situated in the wheat-growing Argive plain. Homer despised the fisherman and the merchant. Homeric heroes were on poor terms with the sea. That society was not yet fully Mediterranean. For it is sea-commerce that will make the lands you touch so essentially lands, separate lands, self-sufficient yet in intercourse, fronting the common waters like the rooms of a Mediterranean house upon its courtyard: it is sea-commerce, rather than land-commerce, which suggests that element of rotation, of hither and thither and definite position which saves each coast or country from being forlorn, from being a mere step to some further horizon: it is sailors who best discover the character and communion of each place. For they do not first consume the land by traversing it: where they strike shelter is their haven.

The idea of a fearless or sane intercourse between man and Nature fostered and was fostered by a life of trade. There is something 'reasonable' about the Mediterranean climate and about the varied and independent communities which that limestone geography harboured.[1] In this smallness of scale, man gained the courage to manoeuvre natural forces, to be inventive. We can use the strategy of Thermopylae and Salamis for our par-

[1] Incidentally one may note that Phoenician trading stations, unlike the Greek, were never situated in land-locked harbours. The Phoenicians preferred a promontory or island site. They feared the narrows would be turned against them; they feared the Mediterranean geography. But we cannot estimate how much Mediterranean civilization, as we conceive it, owed to the Semitic

The Mediterranean

able. The coast line of Hellas is the most varied in the Mediterranean, the most indented. Into the narrows of Salamis the ships of Hellas inveigled the Persian Armada. What an image of the European spirit the Salamic situation provided and provides! For here the moderate and the few lured the oriental hordes into pellucid creeks of a small-scale landscape, engineered the Greek salvation on which, in that clear light, the surrounding cities looked.

In Mediterranean agriculture their exists a constant manipulation of enterprise and care. Unlike the farmers of the Egyptian or Mesopotamian kingdoms who relied absolutely upon the huge perennial flooding of their earths by masterful rivers, the Mediterranean farmer needed, then as now, to labour the year through in his more varied work, sometimes utilizing irrigation to correct the waywardness of the rains. His produce and his diet were in contrast with the continental sameness: the conditions of his farm were likely enough different from those of the farm adjoining. When, finally, a large-scale political unit was firmly established in Mediterranean lands, its strength lay in the degree in which it was an enforced bond of communion between different peoples. The Roman empire was founded upon free trade and other ruthless but practical doctrines.

In ancient geography, Egypt was rightly classed with

races, since we know so little about them. They were the enemies of the Greeks and the Romans through whom our knowledge of the Ancient World has been principally transmitted. There is no doubt that the Greeks learned their seamanship from the Phoenicians whose skill and daring they never equalled. The Greeks assigned the creation of the alphabet to the Phoenicians.

The Mediterranean

Asia. For the geographic conditions of Egypt are Asiatic. The life of Egypt depended upon the almost mechanical gift of the Nile waters. The rivers of Asia sustain their millions or let them die. In the Orient the machinery of Nature and of religion go hand in hand: as when industrial mass machinery breaks down, so, when Nile, Euphrates, Ganges or Yangtze withhold their waters, catastrophe is widespread. Nature in the East is more robot-like than in the West. The Oriental, so far as that term implies a quality, is the natural robot among men. He is blameless of vulgarity, since he is at one with a Nature too mechanical to be pertly questioned. The Roman empire took more than a tinge of orientalism that but heightened Roman vulgarity. For Rome never became an oriental power, for all her wealth and slaves. The slave labour at the command of an Egyptian king, on the other hand, almost took the place of actual machinery. Such were not the conditions in which actual machinery would be developed beyond a certain point. Not that any ancient peoples were interested in mechanics beyond a certain point, except for toys and for the purposes of hieratic miracles. Yet the germ of even modern inventiveness existed in the small-scale character of Mediterranean conditions, which, when the oriental no longer threatened (after the Persian wars), but still was envied, gave rise to the large-scale but non-religious control of the Romans. Mediterranean man became the type of inventive man, the would-be controller of natural forces, more or less conceived as such. And however vast that control has now become, we owe it in the first place to the smallness of the Mediterranean unit, to that climate and geography whose light and contour gave to man, whose cultivation demanded of him, a well-sustained courage and good sense.

Our attention again focuses on the Greek cities. For, compared with Greece, the geographic conditions of Italy are large-scale; compared with Greece, Sicily is easy, fertile. There is a certain buoyancy in the Greek references to that island. There are, of course, rich soils in Hellas. The wheat of Boeotia, for instance, was one of the heaviest in the Mediterranean region. According to Pliny, it was second only to the wheat of Clusium, the best in the world. Attica, on the other hand, was the poorest soil of Hellas. To the envious Athenians, the Boeotians were a byword of stupidity as well as of gluttony. Attica, in contrast, possessed the sublime yet meagre conditions that were the spur to Mediterranean genius. Along the Aegean coasts, particularly in the neighbourhood of Attica, are situated the bottle-necked harbours, the narrows, sands and bays that were the ideal small centres of ancient commerce. Here is the lucid semi-barrenness between the blues of sea and sky, here the thin limestone soils that require so much labour for their shapely fruits and aromatic trees. Here were grown the heavy wines which, stoppered in goatskin, proved to be an emulsion harsher yet more bountiful than the sweet prosaic products of blacker, richer earths.

Where crops depend almost entirely, or entirely, upon irrigation, the size of each agricultural holding will tend to be large. And since the varied growths of Mediterranean cultivation have always needed the maximum care, since that cultivation was, and still is in many respects,

71

The Mediterranean

the most intensive in the world, Mediterranean farms and estates have always tended to be small. Judging from the yield of his farm, a person who was considered to be a great landowner in the time of Solon probably had either 75 to 125 acres of grainland or 20 to 25 acres of vineyard or 50 to 75 acres of mixed land. Agricultural estates of that size in other parts of the world would hardly have been the source of immense riches. Alcibiades was accounted to be a very rich young man when he inherited 70 acres of mediocre soil. Cincinnatus was ploughing his estate of two acres and a bit[1] when he was summoned to be dictator of Rome in 458 B.C. Suetonius tells us that 20,000 Roman citizens were settled in the early years of the Empire on 50,000 jugera (approx. 32,150 acres) of public land between Capua and the Stellas plain. As Miss Semple remarks, "Figures like these, compared with colonial grants in modern Africa and the Americas, illuminate the whole question of agricultural methods and arable area in the Mediterranean lands." These methods, the outcome of Mediterranean conditions, will, at one time or another, breed self-dependent individuals who are yet not the broadest highlanders. There have been other free and independent men, but those of the Mediterranean loved dispute: they found even talking to be an art. To them Europe owed the faint yet immortal democratic idea. However

[1] One thinks at once of the modern fair-sized suburban garden. As it happens, window boxes, too, were a feature of ancient Rome (Seneca, *Epistolae*, 122). But, as between the Mediterranean and the English holding, what a difference it makes that in the South one may grow one's very culture, one's own figs and wine and oil (serves as butter), even though in lieu of many 'choice' suburban vegetables.

The Mediterranean

many serfs were used in Greece and in Italy, however
huge the Roman power, yet the fact remains that the
political nucleus of that civilization to which we have
belonged, lay with the associations of 'responsible',
voluble men. That, of course, might be true of all civilizations. But in Europe, one feels, this nucleus has never
been entirely overlaid by the machinery of vast states
and vast religions.

" Indirect testimony", says Miss Semple, "to the intensive character of ancient Mediterranean tillage is
furnished by certain maxims that embodied old agricultural standards. The ideal was the small freehold estate,
cultivated with infinite care under the master's personal
supervision. The Judean national dream was every man
established on a bit of land where he could rest 'under
his own vine and his own fig tree', when the day's work
was over. . . . The economy of national wealth and the
gain in national efficiency were incalculable. There was
no economic leakage incident to supporting the rural
labour in idleness during half the agricultural year; for
Mediterranean conditions of climate and relief rendered
possible a vegetative year of twelve months. Therefore
Varro and Xenophon show the ancient farmer with his
slaves hurrying from one urgent agricultural task to another. Harvest followed fast upon harvest all through
summer from April to October; and the October harvest crowded upon the heels of the autumn ploughing
and sowing. The days of plenty predicted by the pro-
phet Amos, 'when the ploughman shall overtake the
reaper and the treader of grapes him that soweth seed',
describes the ideal of productive activity in farm life,

73

not only in Palestine, but in other Mediterranean countries. Thus under the prick of Nature's goad, primitive society in these lands began early to develop a capacity for sustained labour, which was at once evidence and guarantee of rapidly advancing civilization."

The richer soils were sometimes used only for grain crops. But every Mediterranean farm wanted and wants to raise bread, oil and wine. Winter is the main season of growth, an opposite condition to that of the Mesopotamian plains whose irrigation depended upon the spring and summer melting of the Armenian snows. Egypt and Babylon were largely spared the endless toil of plowing, harrowing, hoeing and fertilizing. Even in summer months the Mediterranean peasant is occupied: and with autumn he prepares to sow again. With the first autumn rain, Virgil remarks, it was customary to "begin and sow the barley fields right into the showery skirts of frost-bound winter".[1]

In the time of Lycurgus, barley bread and barley stew, cheese, fruit and wine, constituted the free public meals at Sparta. Mediterranean food is not of the kind that inevitably means beautiful plastic receptacles.[2] Barley stew, for instance, does not make the eater conscious of his bowl as does a mould of rice grains or as

---

[1] 1st Georgic, 210-11.

[2] Still, the invention of the fork in the late Middle Ages has probably meant more household everyday ugliness than can be ascribed to any other single cause. For when one eats with fingers or chopsticks it is necessary to *hold* the receptacle near the face. Since thus it is held the eater is most conscious of the receptacle's meaning. It will probably be a bowl, lovely and convenient to the touch, lavish to the mouth, deep to the eye. If we ate without forks we would not stomach common crockery.

does the clear amber of tea. On the other hand, except
for the grain stew or its more modern macaroni equiva-
lent, the Mediterranean meal tends to have the definition or vividness for which the olive gave the standard.
That sharpness conduces especially to eating *al fresco*,
and perhaps in public. As we eat them today in Mediterranean lands, cooked fish still swims, though in oil.
Meat is served surprisingly dry like the rock to which the
goat was tethered. Wine redoubles the expansiveness of
air: so that while *this* thing is affectionately close to the
hand, there is also exultation from the wideness of the
world. . . .

Comparatively speaking, then, the diet of Mediterranean peoples has been a varied one. This was a result
of the intensity of cultivation. One crop was sown to enhance another, and was itself enhanced; a legume sown
among grains, for instance. It is true that farm slaves in
Attica and many parts of Italy were fed on figs, and
almost nothing else, from the summer solstice until late
in the autumn. But, on the whole, compared with the
oriental masses who fed from a more mechanical or uniform tillage, even the poorest Mediterranean peoples
were more vividly aware that there are degrees and
qualities in sustenance. Diversity is a key-note of Mediterranean production. Viticulture may serve us as a
symbol. The many attentions that vines require is in
direct contrast with the monotonous need of date palms,
for instance, which are always contented with the stupe-
fying state of having their heads in the fire of the sun and
their feet in water.

It is perhaps worth stressing that the Mediterranean

The Mediterranean

tillage as we know of it from Theophrastus or Virgil or from those sayings of Mago, the Carthaginian, which have come through to us, was intensive in the modern or scientific sense. Our science adds little to the methods, as opposed to the appliances, of traditional Mediterranean agriculture. Dry farming and irrigation were well developed, also fertilization. For instance, the use of the caprifig or wild fig,in which gall wasps were generated that would fertilize the half-grown domestic fig, was described by Theophrastus. Without chemistry the ancients learned how to conserve the important chemical elements of farm manure: their estimates of the values of various manures are rarely in conflict with modern judgment based upon chemical analysis. The ancient knowledge and carefulness were no doubt prompted by difficulties in obtaining a copious supply of manure. For during the summer four months' drought, cattle and flocks were in highland pasturage, away from the farm. In view of such complexity, no wonder that Theophrastus was tempted to describe with one sentence the tillage of the Tigris alluvium: "Cultivation of the land (in Mesopotamia) consists in letting the water lie on it as long as possible, so that it may deposit much silt."[1]

Marbles and limestones of glowing, diffused and equal light, have underlain the Mediterranean scene as I have described it. For this stone, itself a link between the organic and inorganic worlds, plays a decisive part in determining the humanistic attitude of man to Medi-

[1] *De Historia Plantarum*, viii, 7, 4.

terranean Nature. Those inlets and harbours, dear to
commerce, are mostly of limestone formation. Limestone contour necessitates the small and independent
communities. Vine, olive and fig flourish on limestone
soils. But, so far, the sculptural clarity of that stone, the
Mediterranean light upon it, appear to be no more than
the setting for classical art. My further intention, however, is to represent limestone as dictating no less a content than the forms of that art. Thus, for the sake of
Agostino's sculpture in the Tempio, I shall let it be seen
how intimate and how ancient is the association between images of limestone and of water. So this equation between a basic content together with the basic
forms of classical architecture-sculpture, and the common material in which they were realized, is the first
and most important step of my interpretation of Agostino's marbles. In the Tempio reliefs Mediterranean
life has complete expression: there, water is stone.

What is the source and the strength of this imagin-
ary identification between water and stone? We must
examine in some detail the Mediterranean climate,
especially the rainfall; we must attend to some myth-
ologies and images to which those conditions gave their
form and, in part, their content.

"The significant characteristic of the Mediterranean
climate", says Miss Semple, "is not the amount of the
rainfall, but the fact that the rain is nearly confined to
the colder months of the year, while the summers are
relatively dry. The Mediterranean lands form a region
of winter rains and summer droughts.

"The dearth of rainfall in summer and the relative

abundance in winter is due to the location of the Mediterranean Basin between two regions of sharply contrasted precipitation. It lies on the northern margin of the trade wind or desert tract of Africa; and on the southern margin of the prevailing westerly winds, which all year round bring rain from the Atlantic to northern and middle Europe. The Mediterranean Basin occupies a transition zone between the two, and partakes in turn of the climatic character of each according to the season of the year. In summer it approximates to the arid conditions of the Sahara; in winter it reproduces the stormy skies and frequent rains of France and Germany."

It is worth remark that owing to the potency of our Mediterranean heritage this condition corresponds to our own unconscious standard of what is normal as climate, a condition of sodden winters, of a definite spring, of long summer suns. This is the standard by which we judge the vagaries of our own climate to be vagaries, to be but weather. We expect, entirely without reason, the full southern drama of the seasons. The Gulf Stream that mitigates our northern position allows us at least to hope for Mediterranean days. But whereas we possess a belt of warm foreign waters, Mediterranean lands gain similar benefit from their own sea. "The winter climate is mild. This fact, combined with the winter rains, makes the cooler half of the year the season of plant growth, both for natural vegetation and field crops, while the dry summer is the period of rest. The growing season in general is a long one, lasting from the warm humid autumn favourable for germination through the cool spring to the warm summer, which even at Rome begins before the end of May. Plant life is quiescent at the height of winter in January and through half of February. There are numerous bright clear days in winter which make the sun effective in stimulating vegetation. Athens has 200 days annually with skies entirely clear or merely flecked with clouds, and only 93 days on which rain falls heavily for a few hours as a rule, and then gives way to brilliant sunshine. The mild rainy winters therefore form the climatic basis of Mediterranean agriculture, and assure to this favoured region an adequate and varied food supply not obtainable by a system of summer tillage by irrigation."[1]

The extent of rainfall, however, is extremely variable. In 1883, rainfall at Athens was 34 inches, in 1898 4.5 inches. "This also is characteristic of the Mediterranean climate, resulting in failing springs, exhaustion of water reserves, and ultimate famine. Jerusalem, with a mean annual rainfall of 26 inches, saw its precipitation fluctuate from 43 inches in 1877 to 12.5 inches in 1869. In a period of 60 years it fell twelve times below 20 inches so critical for grain crops, and as often exceeded 32 inches. Years of heavy rains do not bring commensurate benefit to field and pasture, because they are attended by violent downpours and rapid run-off, so that the soil soaks up relatively little of the moisture."[1]

"Annus fructum fert, non tellus," said the Romans. "The seasons produce the crop, not the soil." "The Clouds are our only goddesses: all the rest our bunk," wrote Aristophanes.[2] He thus expressed the perennial Greek anxiety about the autumn and spring rains upon

[1] Semple, *op. cit.* [2] *The Clouds*, 365.

which cultivation largely depended. But the sense of Aristophanes' dictum could be applied to the popular side of all pagan religions in countries whose tillage depended on rainfall, whether in the Old World or the New World. For 'pagan' means 'belonging to the countryside' (paganus): it infers that there exist towns and a settled state of society founded upon tillage. Pagan gods, in the strict sense, are civilized fertility gods: and whereas the sun and the earth symbolize the principle of fertility, in warm yet temperate climates the intermittent and tangible gift of rain would seem to be the more likely object of popular, untutored, but would-be practical, invocation. Especially is this true of Mediterranean lands whose peoples were intensely practical and whose popular religions were the most truly pagan. Compared with fertility religions in other parts of the world, Mediterranean pagan beliefs of historic times were informal: they were less compulsive, less strained in their poetry, less harsh. Rain was symbolized by gods and goddesses of human stature, gods that, for choice, were irresponsible rather than ruthless. To realize the degree in which Mediterranean paganism expresses a more pliant poetry, one need only compare Jupiter with an Aztec rain-god, with the Tlalocs, for instance, on behalf of whose good favours young children were habitually sacrificed weeping. In the interests of sympathetic magic it was important that they should die wet with tears.[1]

[1] Human sacrifice was by no means unknown in Mediterranean lands. But in Greece and Italy, at any rate, it was rare and sporadic and swiftly superseded by offerings of animals. Generally speaking, human sacrifice played no part in Mediterranean culture.

The Mediterranean

As well as Jupiter, Jehovah was primarily a rain-god, also Baal and Zeus and even the Hittite Tesub with whom Baal Casius of the Orontes river was related. For due to their common character as dispensers of rain, all such local Baals and Zeuses and Jupiters were easily mingled and interchanged.

The withholding of rain in Palestine was associated more with man's guilt than in Greece. Compared with other Mediterranean deities, Jehovah was a most jealous god. But the gods of Asia Minor in general were more severe than those of Greece and Italy. These Asiatic gods more frequently required human sacrifice. Palestine itself abuts on deserts that bury blithe values carried from sparkling islanded seas. It is on the edge of the Mediterranean basin, lies open, it would seem, to attack by fierce and bottomless continents. Betwixt plenty and dearth as the heavens dictated, one side caressed by Mediterranean airs, the other side assaulted by the continental animus, the Jews forged from their anxieties a unique doctrine of their own importance. But it was the Mediterranean part of their climate that allowed them to systematize their already developed racial power. They had brought Jehovah with them into Palestine: under those Mediterranean influences that favour man's projection of himself, Jehovah grew to greater lengths his cleansed and cleaning beard. Rain comes from above, a compelling symbol of divine beneficence: while the drought, the high passing of clouds that do not relent or open their rich, pursed lips to drop one drop over their three or four, become a compelling symbol of divine wrath and inspired punishment.

The Mediterranean

The pagans, the Greeks especially, had a more lovely animation: their skies were not as relentless, as extreme. In Greece they trusted the vernal thunderstorms to fortify wheat and barley fields against the approaching drought of summer. All the same, "throughout the Hellenic world from Ionia to Sicily, and especially on the dry eastern side of Greece, supplications ascended to Zeus for the life-giving rain. On the Acropolis of Athens was an image of Earth (Γῆ) imploring Zeus with uplifted hands. The Attic prayer in time of drought has come down to us: 'Rain, rain, dear Zeus, upon the grainlands of the Athenians and upon their pastures.' Zeus controlled every sign of coming showers, such as the autumn lightning that heralded the end of the dry season. Athens had an altar to Zeus, Dispenser of Lightning, where for three months priests kept watch, looking northward towards Mount Parnes for the first flash denoting the presence of the god. When it lightened on the mountain near Harma and Phyle, they sent a sacrifice to Delphi to Apollo, god of agriculture. Pelasgian Zeus the Thunderer had his sacred seat in the oak grove of Dodona in Epiros, on the rainy western side of the Pindus Mountains. There was the earliest shrine of the weather god, where now almost daily thunderstorms occur during June and July, where the annual precipitation is 51 inches and the great Rain-giver abundantly manifests his presence. Thence came the west wind, signalled by the lightning on Mount Parnes, which brought the rare summer thunderstorms to arid Attica.

"The epithets of the Roman god parallel those of

82

The Mediterranean

Zeus. He is Jupiter Pluvius or rainy, Uvidus or wet, Imbricitor or shower-sender, and Serenator or giver of clear weather. He is Jupiter Fulgur or Fulminator in his power over the lightning, and Jupiter Tonitrualis or Tonans as hurler of the thunderbolt. In Greek literature rain was the water of Zeus; so in Roman literature it is frequently the Aqua Jovis or merely Jove, as when Virgil says, 'Now Jove (rain) must be feared for the ripe grapes.' The oak tree, which in its several varieties served as a rain gauge throughout the Mediterranean region, was sacred to Jove all over Italy; oak groves originally surrounded his shrines and temples. Jove it was who sent the fructifying showers upon the thirsty fields and gardens; hence prayers to Jove were a condition of successful tillage. In times of drought, noble Roman matrons walked barefoot in procession up the long slope of the Capitoline Hill to the temple of Jove the Thunderer to pray for rain. So effective were their prayers that 'the rain came down in bucketfuls, and all the women smiled though wet as rats. But now the gods do not come to our help, because we are no longer religious; so the fields lie barren,' says Petronius.

"The original seats of these divine rain-givers—their first rude earthen altars, their shrines and temples were located on hill-tops, mountain summits, lofty peaks, 'the high places of the earth'. These were the 'sacred mounts', like Sinai, Zion, Hermon, Mount Ida of Phrygia and of Crete, Mount Olympos with its cloud-walled city of the gods, that unplaced 'Mount of the Transfiguration', the countless altar-crowned peaks and templed hills of Greece and the Aegean Isles, Sicilian Ætna, the Alban

83

The Mediterranean

Mount with its sanctuary of the Latin tribes, the Capitoline Hill of Rome, and hundreds more wherever they lifted their heads above the wave-lapped shores of the Mediterranean. It was perhaps some deathless memory of this ancient mode of thought, lingering in the folk mind, that made tradition place the sanctuary of the Holy Grail on Mont Serrat, rising from the Spanish shore of the Mediterranean and looking eastward towards that sunrise of the Christian faith on Mount Calvary.

"What was the cogent reasoning that made men of all the Mediterranean world see in these lofty seats the dwelling-places of the Most High—that made Jew, Trojan, Greek, Lydian, Roman and Carthaginian erect thereon the first rude shrines or altars of the rain-gods, and mount these long slopes with prayers and offerings in times of drought?

"Below in the treeless plains a glare of light from cloudless skies, a merciless sun beating down on shrivelled crops and vineyards, meadows parched and sere, the soil baked and cracked with the heat, watercourses dried up made a whole world athirst. Above on the heights clouds rested, and gathered at times for local storms, creating islands of moisture in a vast sea of aridity. There under a grey canopy, refreshed by showery afternoons and dewy nights, grew forests of oak and tamarisk, of chestnut and ash and cedar—sacred groves of all 'high places', handiwork of the Rain-giver, evidence of his presence in this place of his abode. From these tree-grown slopes perennial springs sent their gift of water down to the irrigation ditches in the plains be-

84

low. Even in summer those misty summits held out promise of rain, elusive though it might be; towards the end of the dry season their gathering clouds and the increasing play of lightning were harbingers of the autumn showers. Therefore when the Mediterranean peasant saw his meadow parched by the pitiless sun, his crops dying for lack of water, his irrigation stream shrinking to a trickle and his well or cistern giving out, in despair he looked towards the mountains for sign of rain: 'I will lift mine eyes unto the hills whence cometh my help.'

"There the rain-god manifested himself by clouds, thunder, lightning, and storms. The groves which crowned the dewy summits became his sanctuary, and hence they were marked by rude altars, rarely by temples, because the sites were too remote from the haunts of men. The sanctuaries were often associated with nearby springs and wells, reminiscent of the older worship of the gods of the underground waters; and these waters figured in the cult of the rain-god as another sign of his presence. Such was the spring at the high place of Tarnaach on the north slope of Carmel near Megiddo, and the bell-shaped cistern beneath the high place of Gezer on a western spur of the Judean plateau; and such were the springs and cavern streams that figured in many mountain sanctuaries of Zeus and Baal and Jove."[1]

This, of course, is only one aspect of pagan religion, but one that is prominent because it is symptomatic of many trends in Mediterranean culture. Much of the

[1] Semple, *op. cit.*

The Mediterranean

psychological implications also, of mountain and rain, of stone and water, as perennially associated ideas, do not concern us. It has been sufficient for our purpose to show merely why their association was so vivid in Mediterranean countries. But the extensive variation and pliancy of the drama imputed to stone's relation with water, the classic vividness of the rain myth, was due, I contend, not only to the conditions of Mediterranean climate, but also to the limestone contours of that region, to the underground waters, those older gods, to the springs and ducts which limestones allow; to the more signal, the more exciting, the more varied sculpture that rains create from limestone. In each locality the form of a certain hill or mountain assumed in men's minds a breathing and bountiful power which could command the glistening rains. The carved white marble was not only the image of the god but the god himself. Olympus was not merely the seat of the gods: its vales, its rivulets, the groves and springs, the caverns, the reeds, those winds and rains, those peaks, head and brain to all the limbs, were themselves the gods.

Stone was identified with the god and with the rain. And if we now remember other things that have here been said about limestone in relation to water, the distributed supply to which it lends itself, the chemical response to water upon which an imaginative content has been built, its organic origin from the sea; if we remember the glow of the light upon a pure limestone, like the glow of flesh; if we remember the ease and perfection of its fracture, if we have gathered the impression of such a ratio obtaining between man and Mediterranean

Plate 3. Relief of angels: Agostino di Duccio (Perugia, San
Bernardino).

Plate 4. Flank of the Tempio. Designed by Alberti.

nature as will influence the artist to represent natural forces as idealized human forms: then we may understand how mere marble men and women could be works of art and could be deities, why the waters of springs were gathered deep and clear in marble shrines; why fountains of limestone, colonnades of limestone, baths of pillared hues and crystalline cooling depths, porticoes of deep shadows reverberating like wells, are common in classical art; why spurs of hills were templed, temples clarid, measured, with architraves as smooth as brimming troughs, with entablatures smoothed, divided, notched, put into degrees like the waters above and below sluice-gates; why, in effect, in all stone-work typically Mediterranean there is somewhere expressed the identification or mutual consummation of limestone and water, there is expressed water made solid, permanent, glowing instead of glassy, set in space and brightened by the dripping rains. Water, they say, finds its own level. Each of the blocks that compose a Greek temple rests level on what one feels to be its ideal bed.

A stone shrine about the pool showed worshippers the purity and depths of welded, peaceful, rains. To a degree to which no other culture has attained, the external thing, the objective, concrete, thing in its form of the glowing limestone, became for Mediterranean man the symbol of realized expression. Time or succession appeared to be summed in stone form as homogeneous concrete matter. The clear shapes of mountainous limestone appeared to attract the passing, ephemeral, clouds. Conversely, those solid shapes of stone, those unalterable intervals between peak and peak, were enhanced and dramatized by this passage: while the worshippers who in swarms sought a temple for the promise of rain, in themselves suggested, and were meant to suggest, the raindrops that do not pass beyond marble mountains but drop to lave the stones. This was an analogy for one of the most profound characteristics of classical architecture, the stone architecture built as is no other for the effects of human passage.

Few kinds of building gain anything from the presence of human beings for whom, of course, they exist. Anyone who has been struck by the enhanced beauty of an empty theatre will know what I mean. A dense crowd, of course, may obscure any structure. But in the case of most buildings, however vast, a handful of moving people detracts somewhat from architectural effect. One person may be useful to give the scale, but otherwise even he is generally *de trop*. His movement may contradict the movement or rhythm that the building expresses. A group of persons walking inside or outside a Gothic cathedral cut the soaring stones to pieces with their puny strides. But whereas your movements within it obscure Covent Garden Opera House, as you walk away your passage will enhance the classical portico of St. Paul's, Covent Garden. Even a paper bag blowing in gusts at night between the majestic pillars helps their endowment of proportion, elucidates the incontrovertible spaces between them. For the pillars are, as it were, concreted space; and walking human beings on whose proportions the stone proportions have been founded, or other moving objects which pass across the architec-

tural members or stop between them and thus create a
significant interval, reveal the builded stones' immutable
relationships. We can never see Greek temples as they
were meant to be seen, quite apart from the destruction
they have suffered of their more transient adornments.
In a more profound sense they want their completeness;
their steps, their porticoes want the flashing gait and the
young, garlanded head. They want the slow climbers to
their hills and promontories.

Let us attempt to tighten this relationship between
stone and water and visual art, in Greece especially; so
that, in concluding the first part of the book, we may
return to Venice, our starting-off point, with a new perception.

When we realize that to the classic Mediterranean
mind, contemplation of spring or bouldered stream in a
clear light and amid a sculptural relief, amid a fragrant,
semi-arid wild vegetation, suggested the water content
that found expression in worship and in myth, we pro-
ceed at once to the importance of stone, the channel or
container of fresh water, as well as the bulwark against
the sea.

First the sea. In the Aegean there are many islands of
marble. Except for death with his strangling curtain,
there is nothing so complete in life as where the cliff
stops the sea; at least to him who comes across it. The
earth most palpably begins in the form of rock. Conversely, rock holds, conserves in its purity, embeds the
crystal rains. Limestone is concreted ocean, a concretion of sea-life: marble is a compressed form of lime-

The Mediterranean

stone. Limestone is the common stone of the Mediterranean: it is limestone that runs to rifts and faults, to karsts, to underground channels, to holes and natural pillars, to caverns, to every formation that secretes the cold fresh water, revealing sudden springs and inexhaustible outlets through the dog days. It is limestone,with its power to assume a general glowing light, that gives the certain contour, the shape which, in turn, perfects the shape of cypress or juniper growing there. The yellowing silver of the limestone passes into the filigree olive leaves. Stones and water make the soil. As pre-eminently in Attica, olive and fig flourish on thin limestone soil where rock skeletons are everywhere prone to thrust themselves through the meagre envelope. Moss and bramble, moss-stain and the light or black evergreens, merge themselves with the warm and naked marble or limestone. It is the stones and water that make the soil. Shapely fruits come of its nakedness, fig, olive and grape. It is the light upon the stone that gives the elements each a form, a stature like a man; that shapes each cycle of reasonable fruition. The stone temple fosters a sacred flame: stone also harbours the clear pool, underlies the humus, and conserves it from attrition; for man carves the hill into stone terraces; he stockades the sheep and houses himself: and so the perfectly joined and gleaming temple is the focus for every elemental force. It is the geometric organization of bedrock.

Thus we have the clear land and the clear sea and the varied diet, sea-stone that stops the sea and conducts fresh water: we have the grape, the olive and the fig, and marble gods. We have people who can navigate.

Plate 5. Capricorn.

Plate 6. Venus.

The Mediterranean

Mountain relief and intense commerce mean small and lively communities. They mean also that men for the most part go on foot. Limestone relief provides little pasturage. Among the classical Greeks, only the Thessalians habitually rode. The horse was loved in classical Greece as in Homeric Greece, but he was little more used in daily life than he is to-day. This is very important.

Everything appears different to the man habitually on horseback. It raises him up, makes him wear different clothes, makes him a centaur. In the *Politics*, Aristotle attributes the strong oligarchy that always ruled in Thessaly to the horses, to the advantage, moral and physical, they gave to richer people. The continual use of horses is a barbaric splendour—in the Greek sense of barbaric—a meaning which suggests extravagant or miasmic horizons as if Space moved, or, instead of being the medium in which things stand, could be devoured like Time. Certainly the horseman feels that he devours Space. The ground totters past him. He is an upstart creature, the lover of princes and gaunt ceremony. The poor man is, to him, a biped, a dust-treader. The horseman takes his nobility from the horse. The mountains rear for him, they do not stand. He scatters the stones or curses them.

But those who love stone are those who polish stone, who tread it: those who have loved space have least annihilated it.

Nearly all the principal Greek gods and goddesses had their promontory aspect; that is to say, their temples were built on the promontories most difficult to navi-

gators, for the propitiation of the sea. Poseidon, of
course, had many temples so placed. As we turn Cape
Sunium we can watch to-day Poseidon's temple on the
point. The upright pillars organize the cliff, a whiteness
between the blueness of sky and sea. Or, as at Segesta,
amid the young, folded hills, a temple stands command-
ing the far-flung sea. The position of the stones, the
beam between two uprights, the rise of the stout Doric
shaft uninterrupted from the pavement, the huge smooth
stones rubbed to their perfect jointure, in fact the whole
structural plan of Greek temples, Doric, Ionic, Corin-
thian, was an organization of the landscape, there upon
the hills, an organization that owing to the ratio obtaining between man and his environment achieved perfection and sufficiency without loss of reference to the
human stature. The temples stabilized the country; and
they were symbols of stabilization to men who valued it
most, not only because of the sculptural mountains in
that light, but because they had seen the earth gape, the
alluvial strips disappear and the sea rush in. The fault
line and fracture, the graben and flooded rift valley, due
to Quaternary subsidence, that created the Aegean and
separated Greece from Asia Minor when man was
already evolved, cause this region to be a special earthquake zone: and worship of Poseidon, as the earth-
shaker, was carried far up the unsteady slope of Mount
Parnassus. Sicily, but not Italy, belongs to this violent
tract. We see one reason why the more acrobatic Roman
architecture from which Baroque developed, why the
arch, even, were contrary to Greek values. The Greek
architectural members needed to afford the maximum

effect of steadfastness. On the other hand, volcanoes were unknown in the Aegean except for Methana headland and a few small islands. The smoking mountain, if not common in Italy (and Vesuvius was not active before the Pompeian eruption in 49 A.D. though the mountain of Ischia, now defunct, was always active in classical times), at any rate had been common enough, particularly in Campania, Latium and Tuscany, to cover large parts of the country with volcanic earths retentive of moisture. Whereas the earthquake does not provide a theme in building, except possibly by contrast, volcanic eruptions, though no less fearful, though often accompanied or preceded by earthquakes, stimulate constructive images, perhaps in virtue of the substances that the cones eject and cast about the countryside. In one sense the heat, the flames, the overlaying lava is a richness to the mind. There exists always the tendency to play with fire if only to make a test of one's anxiety and of the danger. *Parturiunt montes*. The mountain wrestles with its burden. The smoking peak is as suggestive of Baroque effect as is the incident in the Roman feast of Fontinalia when the populace threw garlands into the marble fountains. The Greeks standardized their space. One aspect of the Italic genius broke up, reduplicated, extolled space. Nothing is more Italic than the Greco-Roman garden of Sallust at Pompeii, built in the second century B.C. It is only 60 feet long and 20 feet wide, but possesses in suitable scale all the traditional elements of the Mediterranean garden, a fountain, a triclinium, a flower-bordered path. *The rear wall was frescoed to simulate a garden and thus extends the apparent*

93

The Mediterranean

space. We recognize the ingenuity which achieves its maximum expression in Renaissance and Baroque perspective tricks.

Limestone is the very material of classical architecture. The Greek temple of limestone or marble is an organization, not only of the Greek rock, but of the soil and the spring ducts and all the fruit that ensues, all the care and labour they have demanded. This immediate kind of building, the distinct mass of column and column and roof, this ordination of shape and void, light and shade, is the order, composed for classical man, of his space and of his light, and of his elements, all of which have their connection with the limestone. The temple is not white against the sky, but golden, a solid tawniness that suggests the strongest concretion of the process by which the grey olive leaf took nurture and dye from the limestone earth. Classical architecture is limestone architecture. The most fanciful, the most poetic and the most obvious connection of limestone with the elements is with water.

Homer speaks of 'caverned Lacedaemon'. Caves and grottoes, lost and disappearing springs, and the sudden meadows dependent upon their reappearance, perpetual rivulets upon mountain summits, fresh waters that appear from the depths of the sea, in fact every kind of water freak and water beauty ordaining the fantastic range and liquid poetry of classical myths, are characteristic of a limestone relief. In summer, fresh water was indeed precious. Water always needed care. The rapid run-off from the mountains saved the Greeks

The Mediterranean

from the abysmal mythology of great rivers, of slow rivers and their regular savagery. In popular myth, the mountain streams that the sun destroyed so early were the children of Niobe slain by the darts of Apollo. Fresh water was dramatic, a swift visitor, often subterranean in his entrances and exits, even submarine.[1] Water was precious and clear, to be gathered, to be worshipped. So the limestone shrine mirrors the deep pool or forms the perennial fountain. What greater beauty than the stone instrument of space set about the clear pool, or dripping with the fountain, what more solid thing for water, for its clearness, its liquidity, than marble? The ideas of marble and water are closely mingled in our minds. This connection not only reflects the influence of Venice, or of stone fountains galore, of grottoes and Baroque and Rococo garden play, of Roman aqueducts and wells and ancient baths: it is deeper, it reflects the whole vast field of Mediterranean building and Mediterranean influence in every country of the earth. And what beautiful things water does to stone, just as stone to water; what varieties are possible to their combination. I write of them throughout these volumes. Quattro Cento art is only one aspect of that preoccupation, the one I find most profound. In Baroque and Rococo, and, indeed, in most develop-

[1] For instance, the people of Aradus took the greater part of their drinking water from the sea. A spring came up between the island and the coast of Phoenicia. The water-carriers would row out and place a lead funnel over the spring from which the water mounted through a leathern hose to the surface. Again, Pausanias describes the copious spring of Deine in the Argolic gulf. Some of these springs well up and dome with their fountains the surface of the sea.

ments of the use of classical forms in southern climates, the alliance between stone and water is more definitely and dramatically, if more superficially, stated. Classical architecture, in the widest sense of the expression, is the stone architecture *par excellence*, for just this very reason: since stone that wants for an imaginative connection with water loses much of its significance. The water content, of course, was only gradually brought out and stressed and even isolated in such extravagance as the Baroque fountain and grotto. The link here is the use to which the Romans put travertine.

In the original classic forms, in Doric architecture, water content is immanent, unspoken: it helps the clearness of those forms to suit both Mediterranean sea and sky and land. The temple was not merely a structure but a limestone structure that people passed or entered. Behind it, historically, was the channel for flowing water and then the small rain-shrines that made their water still and clear and hard and potable.

Greek art and Greek life reveal the original classic attitude. Protestation comes later. There in the South, in Space, architecture has always been the parent art; and consequently far beyond the South, architecture in any grand sense, and stone structure, have been synonymous. This begets a tangle for us in the North, one of the many tangles we inherit from the intrusion of Mediterranean values. For the use of stone in the South was by no means dictated merely by its superior permanence, as it tends to have been in the North.

Some writers claim to prove that the Doric was originally a wood architecture. But it is an entire mistake

The Mediterranean

to view the Doric limestone temple as a wood structure copied in a more permanent and costly material. For the supply of wood is, and was, often limited in the Mediterranean basin. Most Greek states had difficulty in procuring suitable wood to build their ships. They traded for wood. Stone, on the other hand, limestone, was the stuff of many districts. Whatever the origin of the Doric, it soon became a limestone expression, in some sense proclaiming the prevalence of this stone; so that we cannot imagine any profanation by wood within or without the temple. Again, limestone is warm, takes the light: it is the immediate object, the touchable mass object symbolizing the passage of the southern day: and water closely sips the marble.

Refracted light through clear water throws marble into waves, tempers it with many dimensional depths. Hence the poignancy of submerged temples, or of an Aphrodite's marble arm dragged over the clear and elongating pebbles by the nets of Cnidian fishermen.

We approach one aspect of Quattro Cento sculpture. For the Agostino reliefs in the Tempio have the appearance of marble limbs seen in water. From the jointure of so many surfaces as are carved in these reliefs, from the exaggerated perspective by which they are contrived, from the fact that though bas reliefs they suggest forms in the round, we are reminded of those strange elongations of roundness, those pregnant mountings up and fallings away of flatness, those transient foreshortenings that we may see in stones sunk in clear waters, in the marble floors themselves of baths; we experience again the potential and actual shapes of the stone in water, changing its form, glimmering like an apparition with each ripple or variation of light. But whereas we pick the stone out of the tide or tread the bath floor to discover its real shape, Agostino's forms never cease to be potential as well as actual. Yet this suggested potentiality causes no hiatus in the impression they afford. These shapes are definite enough, unequivocal: only they have as well the quality of apparition which, so far from mitigating the singleness of their impact on the eye, makes them the more insistent and even unforgettable. They glow, luminous in the rather dim light of the Tempio. Their vitality abounds. The life, the glow of marble has not elsewhere been dramatized thus. For, by this peculiar mode of bas relief in which forms in the round are boldly flattened out, the pregnant functions imputed to stone in its relation with water are celebrated with all the accumulated force of Mediterranean art. These reliefs are the apotheosis, not only of Sigismondo who built the Tempio, and of Isotta his mistress, but of marble and limestone and all the civilizations dependent upon their cult.

Pregnant shapes of such a kind are possible only in relief carving. We begin to understand how, at its first elaboration, perspective science was the inspiration, the true and deep inspiration, and not merely the means, of Renaissance art; why it was the early Renaissance carvers, rather than the painters, who discovered and elaborated this science. We begin to understand how it is that what I have called Quattro Cento sculpture, with its stone-blossom and incrustation, with its love of stone,

of movement, liquid and torrential movement within
the stone (needing perspective to measure distance),
with its equal love to carve shells and growth and steady
flower, should be considered the core and centre of the
Renaissance. The Renaissance is a gigantic yet concentrated reassertion of Mediterranean values. The diverse
cultures of all the centuries since classical times were
commandeered for this expression, and thus reinforced
the imitation of classical modes, themselves of several
periods. Thousands of years of art were employed in
this furore. But again, the core, the central fury, was
the love of concrete objects. Each diverse Mediterranean feeling for stone found a new vehemence. And
of those feelings of which I write throughout these
volumes, I consider the most fundamental one to be
connected with the interaction of stone and water. In a
sense, the fecund stone-blossom is already connected
with some association of moisture in the stone.

Before coming to Rimini, Agostino probably spent
some time in Venice. We do not know for certain the
history of his development; whether his Tempio man-
nerisms were already a part of his style in Venice,
whether he brought them to Rimini, or whether they
were only then developed, perhaps at the instance of
Sigismondo Malatesta, his patron, whose personality
and whose love the Tempio sculpture relates.

Probably there is no simple explanation of Agostino's
style. It is obvious, though, that Sigismondo was an
important factor. For Agostino's carving expresses his
subject as no other carving could have done. But the

The Mediterranean

fact of Venice must, at any rate, have reinforced Agostino's imagination. And just as a writer can better visualize a place when he has left it, so Agostino turned the spell of Venice to better use at Rimini than he could have accomplished in Venice herself.

It is only right that we should return to the subject of Venice at this point. She is my constant theme. For Venice is the witness of Mediterranean art. Here by themselves are the Mediterranean waters, and the Mediterranean stones each one of them shaped by man.

You might have expected a wealth of marine ornament in Venice. The Venetians, however, were more concerned to suggest ties with the green land. But the sensitiveness to marine effect in the Renaissance must be directly related to the existence of Venice, or, rather, to its becoming, at that time, the Venice we have, city of stone and water, the most stupendous, the most far-reaching of humanistic creation. After all, Venice is the one permanent miracle, and the presence of this miracle in the heart of Europe for fifteen hundred years is an historical factor whose influence is too vague and large for its conceiving by historians. All that we should note here is the gigantic outlay of stone, hiding the Venetian mud, an undertaking, a reinvestment, a transformation the rumour of which passed throughout Italy. Marble palaces are cliffs now as well as houses, and the marble water-stairs run without a break between air and sea, only that the deeper steps lapped and submerged, seem to serpentine, and this movement interrupts on the surface the reflection of a palace opposite; only that the step on a level with the flood, from which

The Mediterranean

there is a dry passage into the cavernous marble hall of a palace, continually rebuts the slap of the tide, and at each pause shows white, wet teeth. The creations only of man and of water, no intermediary, except their fusion by half-visible marble that glimmers below the surface like a sea-serpent; while the stretched and relaxed sea-weed adhesive shows the direction of the tide as a weathercock the point from which the wind comes. A ship has no such fusion with the element it rides. Without conscious effort and without sacrifice of their humanity, the Venetians have come nearer to an element than have done all the races to another element, earth, with various mysteries and nature worship, especially spring and autumnal rite. Without loss of humanity, without dark ecstasy, without priests, they have done it. Such closeness of rational, supremely practical man to Nature is humanistic; and so pervasive is the closeness, that either man or sea animals may well find a home here. Even to-day in this the city of historical commerce created out of business enterprise, though the trappings of several civilizations are vaunted here, it would be little surprise if shading one's eyes when upon the piazzetta, scanning the lagoon that is only inches below the marble floor, one were to see framed between the two columns, twin heads and fast approaching coils, Laocoon's serpents coming over from the horizon in the time that it takes to give a speech, and now breasting up the water-stair between the tattered gondolas. In spite of the ubiquity of their art here as no-where else, human beings, with their staccato movement and perpendicular line, sometimes seem match-stick-like, superfluous. Then one would like the marine animals to take possession. Imagine rows and rows of serpents in horizontal glide across the piazza, not stopping or turning at St. Mark's, but rearing up their wet scales to coil them about the porphyry and serpentine pillars, to lay their eggs in the recesses of the massive foliage of the capitals, to leave their slime upon the porphyry head of Justinian and slither down the sheeted walls. Imagine the already bejewelled palaces of the Lombardi further encrusted with salt and brittle shells, imagine dolphins sporting beneath a bridge, flapping their tails with hollow sound against its steep underside. Along a narrow back canal an improbable monster is paddling, his head reared up on a level with the *piano nobile* so that he spews through windows either flank on to brocaded chairs. Now his head is three canals in advance of his tail, his body is grinding scales in three places against right-angled marble corners. Rank wash rushes up the water-stairs and refloats a flotilla of oozing toads. Seals crease their bodies poised on a narrow pink parapet, down the banisters of the Giants' staircase eels race. A grampus with dripping paws has replaced St. Theodore upon his column and cetacean roars reverberate in the porphyry dingles. Salmon jump a fondamenta, sea-snakes crawl up the sheer sides of every campanile, parti-coloured cuttle-fish staining the pavement black squirm to reach the shoals stranded upon Rialto. The tentacles of giant octopi, like so many hands raised in mysterious benediction, rise out of the lagoon over the façade of Palladian San Giorgio . . . .

Part Two

Stone and Clay

Chapter Four

Carving, Modelling and Agostino

The Tempio reliefs which most concern me and which provide the majority of the illustrations are arranged as follows: lying back an inch and a half or so from a frame of moulding, they constitute, together with this frame, the surfaces on three sides of piers. These piers support arches that form the entrances to chapels. Plates 24 and 37 best illustrate the sculpture's arrangement. The reliefs are for the most part low, yet their forms possess many values of sculpture in the round: while the quickened mass of a human shape between wind-strewn films of drapery, the delicious torture of hair and clothing by an unseen, evocative wind upon the outer and intermediary surfaces of a relief, give to its body the effect of vitality, of that stone-blossom we prize so high. Even carved landscapes by Agostino are restless, even the countryside is drunk with this dithyrambic draught that impels to ecstatic dance as did the breezes in the sybilline cave, scattering the mad leaves of prophecy. In the relief[1] representing

[1] This relief in the Castello Sforza, Milan, has been attributed to Agostino ever since Yriarte noticed it. Ricci has subsequently identified the subject and has shown that it was originally affixed

the journey of San Sigismondo to the monastery of Augauno, a pillar surmounted by the statue of an angel appears among the surrounding mountains like a lighthouse encompassed. Still more in the landscape representing the influxion of the moon, sea and land are mingled in supernal agitation upon which a youth rides in a boat (Pl. 48). At the Tempio, the young Agostino evolved his style; under the influence of his patron, Sigismondo, who aroused choriambic visions, he created his masterpieces. The sea is vibrant with fish, boughs bend under the weight of birds, the active airs breed a flock of doves that descend to greet the new-born Venus from the sea to earth (Pl. 6). The land undulates with vegetables and animal life just as the sea with fish. But his preoccupation with sea-movement—his garments, though ostensibly disturbed by wind, cling to and disclose naked forms like seaweed waving on submerged rocks, or they are like water falling clear as the bather rises to leave the pool—was undoubtedly stimulated by Venice whither he came after leaving Florence. Sigismondo made him—to his presentiment of movement added a sense of spell. A spell was upon the spirit of Agostino, the spell of Isotta[1] communicated to him by his master upon whom it first lay, a spell which,when enlarged over the varying subjects of Agostino's work, brings to mind the afflicting magnetism of the moon that confounds the height with the depths, transforming landscape into the basin of a forgotten sea.

beneath the throne of S. Sigismondo in the chapel of that name in the Tempio. A cast of the relief has now been put there. The original was in the 1930 Italian Exhibition at Burlington House.

[1] Sigismondo's mistress.

Carving, Modelling and Agostino

Thus, though superficially the movement expressed by these reliefs evokes a sense of air currents, yet, as we shall see later more clearly, Agostino's root preoccupation was with water forms and water movement.

But before I try to put into words the crystallization presented by this carving, of the deeper Mediterranean fantasies in connection with limestone, I mean to prospect the whole field of sculpture. Agostino achieved what he did just because he was essentially a carver of limestone, far more essentially so than were the majority of his famous contemporaries, and perhaps more so than any sculptor whose work we have. At the instance of Agostino, then, it will be possible to grasp what is the carving approach as distinguished from the modelling approach. To raise this issue is by no means to embark upon discursion. My sole aim still is to interpret the values of Agostino's sculpture. And since these are bound up largely with the imperfectly recognized virtues of carving pure and simple, so wide an issue must now be discussed for his good. Otherwise he will be appreciated and condemned in accordance with more or less irrelevant standards, that is, in accordance with considerations of plasticity or modelling by which all carving, in whatever material, is to-day largely judged.

The predominant virtues, then, of Agostino's sculpture demand that a basic distinction be made between what is carving conception and what is plastic or modelling conception, even though some traces of both conceptions are to be found in all sculpture whether it be carved or modelled. In view of the Germans and their horrid

107

Carving, Modelling and Agostino

noun *Plastik*, one cannot emphasize too strongly that sculptural values are not synonymous with plastic values. The values in sculpture which find but little expression in modelling are those which have been forgotten. Few people are deeply sensitive to them. Neither the German nor the Italian critics are capable of 'seeing' an Agostino relief, beyond its often indifferent modelling. This state of affairs is intensified by the currency of photographs. Photographs transmit plastic values exceedingly well, carving values hardly at all. At this point my own photographs are a hindrance. The reader who has looked at them may have wondered why I should make so prolonged a fuss about these reliefs. As plastic conceptions, the majority are by no means first-rate. Still, if the reader will follow me through this chapter, I shall offer him the true values of these reliefs in such a way that my photographs may possibly prove an advantage rather than a hindrance.[1]

So we shall now attack the vital though confused aesthetic distinction between carving and modelling. There must be a profound aesthetic distinction between them. As everyone knows, carving is a cutting away, while modelling or moulding is a building up. Agostino's virtue will shed new light upon the high imaginative constructions which common fantasy has placed around each of these antithetical processes: (imagina-

---

[1] The reader, however, must bear in mind that, with the exception of the two Victoria and Albert Museum exhibits, all the carving here illustrated is architectural. The architectural arrangement of the reliefs determines the greater part of their attraction. I must apologize for my failure to obtain photographs that might show them to better advantage.

tion itself is a plastic agency, fashioning its products with fragments). Agostino's virtue will illumine afresh the field of visual art. For the distinction between carving and modelling proves to be most suggestive in relation to all visual art.

The visual arts are rooted in handicrafts. Let us keep the expression 'the Fine Arts'. For these are the useless arts, a development of handicraft that is valued, although the products possess no utilitarian function. They are the superb development of fine objects made for use. And, in turn, the handicrafts are a heightened manual skill grown from the exercise of manual labour as a whole. Every artist has more than a practical interest in labour. Just as plants, worms and insect life turn the soils and help to disintegrate the rock, just as animals crop the vegetation, so the cultivator carves the earth, hoeing and ploughing the ground, cutting the undergrowth, the trees and the planted corn. And just as the cultivator works the surfaces of the mother earth so the sculptor rubs his stone to elicit the shapes which his eye has sown in the matrix. The material, earth or stone, exists. Man makes it more significant. To wash, to polish, to sweep, are similar activities. But to weave or to make a shoe, indeed the processes of most trades, are pre-eminently manufacture, a making, a plastic activity, a moulding of things.

Plastic shape in the abstract is shape in the abstract, while carving shape, however abstract, is seen as belonging essentially to a particular substance. It is obvious that all carving is partly to be judged by its plasticity, that is to say, by the values of its forms apart from consideration of their material. But that approach alone to carving is inadequate and in some cases (Agostino's reliefs for example) is altogether beside the point. It is like judging sculpture by photographs.

Briefly, the difference between carving approach and modelling approach in sculptural art can be illustrated as follows. Whatever its plastic value, a figure carved in stone is fine carving when one feels that not the figure, but the stone through the medium of the figure, has come to life. Plastic conception, on the other hand, is uppermost when the material with which, or from which, a figure has been made appears no more than as so much suitable stuff for this creation.

In the two activities there lies a vast difference that symbolizes not only the two main aspects of labour, but even the respective roles of male and female. Man, in his male aspect, is the cultivator or carver of woman who, in her female aspect, moulds her products as does the earth. We see both the ultimate distinction and the necessary interaction between carving and moulding in their widest senses. The stone block is female, the plastic figures that emerge from it on Agostino's reliefs are her children, the proof of the carver's love for the stone. This communion with a material, this mode of eliciting the plastic shape, are the essence of carving. And the profundity of such communion, rather than of those plastic values that might be roughly realized by any material, provide the distinctive source of interest and pleasure in carved objects.

It was not inappropriate that the tool carved as an

instrument for carving or to cut now a branch, now the skull of an enemy, should have had so masculine a shape. Knapped flints, rubbed obsidians and jades, are most satisfying as carving. The demands of reality and of the connections made by the fantasy are here in simple accord. One might go further. It is from such coincidence that a thus reinforced fantasy has proceeded to create visual art.

This is the point at which to emphasize the pre-eminence of stone as the material to be carved. I am not thinking of its durability, nor even of the shape it will allow. I am thinking of the equal diffusion of light that, compared to most objects, even the hardest and darkest stones possess; I am thinking of hand-polished marble's glow that can only be compared to the light on flesh-and-blood. The sculptor is led to woo the marble. Into the solidity of stone, a solidity yet capable of suffused light, the fantasies of bodily vigour, of energy in every form, can be projected, set out and made permanent. Most other statuary materials, bronze and terra-cotta, are far higher mediums of manifestly reflected lights, as if their light were not their own light. The majority of stones, on the other hand, are faintly or slightly translucent so that their light seems to be more within them. Polishing, when it is hand-polish and not a chemical polish, in nearly every case gives life and light to the stone without causing it to be so brilliant as to lose a great part of its light again in reflecting it, or to be over-confused and deadened by manifestly accepting lights reflected on to it. It is the difference between light and lights. The great virtue of stone is that unlike other hard materials it seems to have a luminous life, light or soul. Limestone in particular blends the virtues of hard and soft materials. Whatever virtues I now attribute to stone in general I have already attributed in particular to limestones and marbles.[1]

Owing to the equal suffusion of light on stone, its most gradual shapes are unavoidable, especially since they are seen in association with stone's solidity: for hardness of material gives an enormous sense of finality to shape. The obsidian that has been thinned yet rounded to a cylinder at the shaft provides one with a far greater sense of roundness than does a ball of clay. The roundness of a flint is so compact, so heavy, its roll so continuous. As for representation of the human form, it will readily be understood that in the carving of stone's hard luminous substance, it suffers all the stroking and polishing, all the definition that our hands and mouths bestow on those we love.

Polishing stone is also like slapping the new-born infant to make it breathe. For polishing gives the stone a major light and life. 'To carve' is but a complication of 'to polish', the elicitation of still larger life. Carving is a whittling away. The first instinct in relation to a carvable material is to thin it, and the first use of such material as tool or weapon required it to be sharp, to be graduated in thinness.[2] The primary (from the imaginative point of view) method of carving is to rub with an

[1] In Chapter II.

[2] I make no reference to gems. When I speak of stone, the glass-like and fragmentary precious stones are never within my vista. Possibly to the imagination they form a subject by themselves, one for which I have little feeling.

abrasive. It is possible that the forms in stone sculpture which possess pre-eminently a carving, as opposed to a plastic, significance, have nearly always been obtained by rubbing, if only in the final process. However, it is not necessary for me to enter into a discussion of technique. I think one can hold that from the deep, imaginative angle, the point, chisel, drill and claw are not so much indispensable instruments of stone sculpture as auxiliary weapons that prepare the stone for the use, however perfunctory, of abrasives. The chisel and the rest facilitate stone sculpture: and, historically speaking, it may be that these instruments were adopted from wood carving and gem carving for this purpose, rather than invented for use on sculptural stone.[1] But the only point I wish to make is that rubbing belongs integrally to the process of stone sculpture. Wood, on the other hand, is never carved by rubbing.[2] Herein lies the fundamental difference between stone and wood sculpture: for it is reflected in the shapes proper to each, whatever be the actual instruments with which they are attained. Stone demands to be thinned, that is to say, rubbed. Wood demands to be cut and even split. Wood is not only not so dense, but possesses less light seemingly its own. Typically wooden shapes are nearer to typically

[1] See *The Technique of Early Greek Sculpture* by Stanley Casson, Clarendon Press, 1933.

[2] This statement is true only in the present context, that is to say, in helping to define a trend or principle. If read literally, it is untrue. Some very hard wood forms—many instances of negro wood sculpture spring to mind—were undoubtedly attained by rubbing. But in these cases the hard wood was treated almost as stone : the basic forms are stone-like, though, to their detriment, they lack stone's even light.

modelled shapes. Hence, wooden shapes need to be more emphatic. In contrast with the flattening or thinning proper to stone more definitely circular shapes are proper to wood, conditioned as well, in the majority of cases, by the rounding tree-growth formation of its grain. But the light on stone reveals the slightest undulation of its surface; and since no stone has a general circular structure, curves depend entirely on the care with which the block has been diminished. Such forms, though they may suggest the utmost roundness, will tend in reality to be more flattened or compressed than in the case of carved wood. Indeed, as we have said, from this lack of exaggeration, from this flattening or thinning of the sphere, the slightest roundness obtains the maximum life and appeal. The light on stone is comparatively even: no shape need be stressed: where complete roundness is avoided, the more it may be suggested. So the shapes proper to stone are gradual, to which sharpness is given only by the thinned nature of the block as a whole.

Carving is an articulation of something that already exists in the block. The carved form should never, in any profound imaginative sense, be entirely freed from its matrix. In the case of reliefs, the matrix does actually remain: hence the heightened carving appeal of which this technique is capable. But the tendency to preserve some part of the matrix is evident in much figure carving, and in the case of some arts, has given rise to definite conventions: thus, the undivided knees of Egyptian granite kings and idols. My example is a literal one: for even though no part of the matrix is palpable, the conception of it may yet be imputed to some part of the form. This is the inspiration behind many of the great hard-stone Egyptian heads. In conception and execution they are pure carving; of which the proof is that nothing, no nothing, is more meaningless, more repulsive, than a plaster cast of one of these heads.

I speak of all stones as if they possessed pre-eminently the light and the texture which, in a previous chapter, I attributed to certain limestones. The majority of stones have these virtues, but to a much smaller degree. It follows that Egyptian hard stones, such as granites, diorites and porphyries, are by no means the most vivid kinds of stone. They lack marble's even and palpitating light. Their extreme hardness and harsh light entail comparatively rounded shapes. Softer stones, on the other hand, tend to be diminished to greater thinness. Their curves, no less gradual, will be more capable of a varied palpitation in their defining of forms. Such definition of form by whittling and polishing marble, so that in representational art the figures themselves tend to be flattened or compressed, as if they had long been furled amid the interior layers of the stone and now were unburdened on the air, were smoothing the air, such thinness of shape appears to me to be the essential manner of much stone carving. This manner, also, preserves for us the influence of the once enclosing matrix.

Superb instances of such shape in its most direct form are provided by the little prehistoric marble figures that come from the Cyclades. Many of these figures are so thinned out that they will not stand up.

Carving, Modelling and Agostino

The heads particularly are squashed back. Yet what roundness is suggested by the curve of the shoulders, what fullness by the slight indication of the breasts! Curiously enough, such sensitiveness to the radiance of human form and to the kindred radiance of marble immediately proposes a Greek ancestry, although these figures antedate Achaian invasions by many hundreds of years. One will conclude, however, that this particular sensitiveness to luminous gradations of marble, Greek or not Greek, is through and through Mediterranean.

I will not stop to consider the direct evidence of such flattening in Mexican sculpture, for instance, nor attempt to elucidate it in all the major sculpture of the world. I shall not otherwise refer to the almost paper-like thinness of the earliest Chinese jades, nor explain how that though granites tend for each section to make for heavily rounded shapes, yet the colossal height of much Egyptian figure-sculptures is itself an elongation that brings them into line with pyramid and obelisk.

I pass straight on to relief. This, I contend, is a dramatized form of carving. The shape is on the surface, the matrix behind it.

It is obvious that in relief carving, especially low relief, flattened or compressed shapes can be shown to the greatest advantage; indeed, the utmost degree of compression can here serve as the direct and constant aim of the carver, an aim to which all stones inspire him. Just as an enhanced feeling of the spherical is attained in stone to the glory of stone, by elongating spheres into ovoids and into other gradually rounded shapes, so three-dimensional form may become all the more

116

Carving, Modelling and Agostino

significant from being represented by the compressed shapes of low relief. Advisedly I say 'can serve' and 'may become'. For, except Agostino, no sculptor known to me has flattened into low relief almost entire figures in the round. Agostino's reliefs are the apotheosis of carving. His isolation, and the moderate approval that his work has won, but indicate how undeveloped, generally, is the emotion that the very idea of stone carving should inspire; or, at any rate, how easily it gives ground to emotions aroused by considerations of plasticity.

I realize that I owe in the first place to the contemplation of Agostino's work all that I feel about stone. No other sculptor can teach so much about carving. His achievement inspires the search for its origins. As my comment, I have needed to range the Mediterranean geography and the character of limestone. For at the time of the Renaissance, above all, it was the inheritance of feeling derived from concrete objects that became intense. Agostino's qualities, of course, were in part shared by some of his contemporaries, certainly in those of their works that I have described as Quattro Cento.

A more definite search for the origin of these qualities than the one I pursue, a definite research in the technique of ancient or medieval reliefs, will explain but little. Assyrian, Mexican and Hittite low reliefs, for instance, show no large degree of flattening. Classical high relief often has the appearance of free-standing statuary that has been cut off three-quarter or half by the background plane. This matrix not only does not assist the carving value but muddles the plastic value.

Carving, Modelling and Agostino

Classical low relief is, essentially, an engraving; in actuality, a raised surface surrounded sometimes by a grooved outline. This contour is clearer from the distance than a general incising of the stone would be. I rarely find a deeper inspiration behind such relief. It is intended that the figure should look as flat as possible on the raised surface. Relief is substituted for engraving merely in the interests of greater clearness. An Agostino relief is exactly opposite in conception and technique. It is intended that the figure should look as round as possible, while the lower the surfaces by which the effect is achieved, the better. So great is the three-dimensional significance of some of the Tempio reliefs, that one needs to touch their surfaces to realize fully the degree of their flatness.

In many periods of art throughout the world, low relief has too often served merely as a raised incision, a drawing or engraving in stone whose sides have been cut away to afford sharpness and definition. No wonder that our more thoughtful contemporary sculptors have no interest in relief!

I shall return to the question of relief. It is time to say something about the nature of modelling.

That with which you model in sculpture is as much a material as the stone to be carved. But plastic material has no 'rights' of its own. It is a formless mud used, very likely, to make a model for bronze or brass. Modelling is a much more 'free' activity than carving. The modelled shape is not uncovered but created. This gives rise to a freer treatment, free in the sense that it is a

Carving, Modelling and Agostino

treatment unrestricted by so deep an imaginative communion with the significance of the material itself. The modeller *realizes* his design with clay. Unlike the carver, he does not envisage that conception as enclosed in his raw material.

If the primary carved shape is an obsidian tool or weapon, the primary moulded shape is a clay receptacle. The unglazed bowl is written with the potter's fingertips: thus he expresses the completeness of its manufacture: while enamelled pattern over glaze and slip, or on porcelain, are an elaboration of his touch, are the potter's written characters. As we shall see, the calligraphic and supremely personal element in graphic art is always to be associated with modelling conception (particularly in the case of oil painting), while painting, for instance, that essentially illuminates a certain space, the use of pigment that is more directed by some architectural conception of planes, is preferably to be classed with carving.

One can say at once of modelling forms (as opposed to carving forms) in the widest sense, that they are without restraint: I mean that they can well be the perfect *embodiment* of conception: whereas, in the process of carving, conception is all the time adjusted to the life that the sculptor feels beneath his tool. The mind that is intent on plasticity often expresses in sculpture the sense of rhythm, the mental pulse. Plastic objects, though they are objects, often betray a tempo. Carving conception, on the other hand, causes its object, the solid bit of space, to be more spatial still. Temporal significance instead of being incorporated in space is

Carving, Modelling and Agostino

here turned into space and thus is shown in immediate form, deprived of rhythm.[1]

Modelling conception, untrammelled by the restraint that reverence for objects as solid space inspires, may run to many kinds of extreme. For instance, on the one hand there are the simple, 'pure', forms of many fine pieces of pottery, exhibiting a purity or completeness in manufacture that is foreign to the very substance of stone: on the other hand there are potential or conglomerate forms that are consciously impressed with the associative and transitional qualities of the mind's processes. The rapid content of Rodin's sculpture and, indeed, of impressionist art as a whole, serves as an example.

Characteristic of modelling is an effect of the preconceived. In any Ting ware bowl, a most complicated thoughtful conception has been realized by a simple shape; while the thrust of some all-absorbing rhythm, simple enough in its fundamental movement, has been realized in virtuoso or masterly style by Bernini, Manet and Rembrandt, in unequivocal or monumental style by Donatello and Michael Angelo. One does not encounter so prominent a masterliness, so 'wilful' a preconception in what is essentially carving. For carving entails a dependence, imaginative as well as actual, upon the material that is worked. The stone block attains vivid life under the hand that polishes. Similarly, the

---

[1] " Objects perceived simply as related in space, encourage the ambition of every man for complete self-expression, for an existence completely externalized. Our love of space is our love of expression." *The Quattro Cento*, Vol. I, p. 158.

Carving, Modelling and Agostino

shape of the material on which Piero della Francesca and even Giorgione painted was of the deepest significance to them, far more so than in the case of Rubens, for instance, or of Vermeer. These latter, in their vastly different ways, were often engaged in such potent modelling that they negatived the picture plane by their compositions, as did all the Baroque painters. Theirs was the supremely personal, the supremely 'aesthetic' touch; theirs the calligraphic omnipotence so characteristic, as well, of far-eastern pictorial art. The Baroque calligraphy was generous, bold, adult: while the Chinese calligraphy, though far more subtle, in painting at least has always been at root an art of precocious childhood, that is to say, cunning and exquisite splodges upon a white surface.

Most developed visual art displays a calligraphic competence. Calligraphy becomes extreme only when a calligraphic draughtsmanship is that to which each of the visual arts approximates. Such was the position in Baroque times. A Baroque church, a Baroque painting, a Baroque sculpture, each of them possess the verve of experienced and rapid handwriting. All unabashed modelling conception may be put into terms of such draughtsmanship, particularly since materials are so interchangeable in modelling. All sculptural modellers should primarily be such draughtsmen. I do not mean merely that they should be able to draw, but further, that their modelling should be but a projection of this primary penmanship. The true carver's power to draw, on the other hand, is a secondary power: for it is inspired by his attitude to stone. He has sought to illum-

Carving, Modelling and Agostino

inate the stone with file or chisel: now he seeks to illuminate paper with pencil or brush, so as to articulate its evenly lighted surface. 'Illuminated manuscripts' are a just description of the painting that springs from this attitude; and to these illuminations, the painting that was inspired by the character of stone always bears some reference. There may be a strictly linear approach to contour; but in the developed pictorial art of this kind, the painter will emulate the tonal values which the actual carver reveals on the surfaces, more or less equally lit, of his block. This painter's employment of tone is distinct from all other employments of colouring: in comparison they are adventitious; whereas the former method gives rise to the painting, whether it be more linear or more 'tonal' in technique, that is most deeply founded upon tonal conception. To my mind, such is the only true painting. There are, of course, all degrees of this profundity. Thus a Piero della Francesca picture causes all nearby pictures to cease as paintings. For, in comparison, they appear to be no more than coloured designs, calligraphic brushwork, tinted drawings.

I shall not risk the further confusion of the reader at this juncture, by following up so difficult a distinction in the realm of painting. This subject, in its entirety, belongs to a subsequent volume. But, so far as it is now necessary to my interpretation of Agostino's carving, I believe it will become clearer in due course.

To turn again to sculpture proper.

I have attempted to isolate the essential carving from the essential modelling. We may now form a better idea of their interdependence. For let me admit at once that in

Carving, Modelling and Agostino

no part of the world has there existed a sustained figure
carving in which modelling did not influence, and so,
extend, the carver's aim; nor have artists with the
strongest plastic preconceptions disliked, for what were
considered monumental works at any rate, the suggestions of carving that result from the execution of their
designs in wood or stone. There is no doubt that in the
majority of developed periods, sculptors have desired to
combine the plasticity of poise and rhythm with those
qualities of a spatial object which, it is felt, can only be
translated and enhanced rather than created. Stone
exhibits these qualities at their highest. And so, plastic
conceptions have been realized pre-eminently in stone
as well as in plastic materials; and that not only because
of the greater durability of stone.

So confused a conceptual admixture, of course, is
foreign to the pure plastic art of Chinese earthenware
and porcelain. But in limestone Europe, the influence of
stone on modelling is evident from the earliest times,
particularly in the South. After the initial rapproche-
ment, so typical of European art, the relationship is
sustained with reversed roles. For the quick development of the more facile process, modelling, then constantly influences the carver. Indeed, one can make the
generalization that the greater the power of carving to
absorb modelling aim, the more incessant will be the
infiltration of plastic values into that carving. *Thus, the
proof of the importance of stone in European art is the prevalence of plastic aim in European carving.* A period comes in
Europe, however, when an excess of plastic aim in
stone-work overpowers the nexus with carving values.

Carving, Modelling and Agostino

As carved stone the resultant product will be empty, though it may still be lovely as modelling; since a successful plastic idea is little bound up with any one material; indeed, its entirety may be suggested by a drawing. But it is probable, since the one defines the other, that when the values proper to carving are finally lost, modelling is atrophied sooner or later. There then intervene those grotesque confusions in aesthetic values such as we attribute to the Hellenistic age and, still more, to our own immediate past. At such a time it is essential to start afresh with the primary values of carving and modelling. This is our position to-day.

At other times European aesthetic values are never clear. It is obvious, however, that some real nexus with stone can survive a far greater infiltration of modelling conception in Mediterranean lands whose art, I have suggested, is based directly upon the character of limestone, than in the northern countries which have emulated so rashly in this respect the Mediterranean freedom. The thousand-and-one marble figures, the Hellenistic statuary, so palpable in realistic modelling, were yet a stone display amid limestone temples, amid grove and courtyard and flowering tub, as they stained themselves with pure water above the fountain, or stood on the sky-line striking the blue with posed yet marble arm. No doubt they are almost meaningless in our northern museums: not so when they stand throughout the sun, or pale against the moon. The Hellenistic statues are poignant by the thousand, and poignant is Cassiodorus' narrative of sacked Rome, populated by 5,000 men and 100,000 ideal marble figures.

Carving, Modelling and Agostino

In the Renaissance, the love for stone gathered so unparalleled a force that the answering infusion of modelling values served to dramatize, in Quattro Cento sculpture at least, the values proper to stone.[1] Under the enormous stress of modelling, however, those values became more and more diffused. In any case, plastic aim was at all times the conscious aim of Renaissance artists. The Quattro Cento spirit, nucleus of the Renaissance, goes on to be little more than the fierce spur to modelling. Baroque then occupies the whole field.

The carving which appeals most to me is the 15th-century carving that not only withstood an enormous infiltration of plastic values, but even employed them to show the measure of its own strength, the love and understanding of stone. This is the Quattro Cento sculpture, so-called in these volumes. Quattro Cento carving is carving triumphant. Yet here again there are degrees. In love and perception of stone, Agostino outstripped all his contemporaries. To demonstrate the extent of his achievement in this respect, we shall later compare a relief by him with one by Donatello. For, compared with Agostino, Donatello himself was a modeller pure and simple.

At this point, in connection with the interdependence of modelling and carving, I perceive that some reference that bears upon the character of naturalistic art is needed. For one may imagine that, in the first place, the Hellenic modeller desired to create a naturalistic figure, not least of all because he was responsive to the flesh-

[1] Hence the popularity in the Renaissance of relief, which, we have seen (p. 116), may well be a dramatized form of carving.

Carving, Modelling and Agostino

like glow of the limestone rocks and buildings and statues about him, and to other humanistic influences of Mediterranean topography which, at some point, are always connected with that living yet objective condition of the stone as I too have conceived it. A plastic idea may vitalize, as well as de-vitalize, carving aim. What a stimulus it must have been to Hellenic carvers when the first naturalistic bronzes were taken from the mould! Here were the figures which the carver had vaguely attributed to his block as the fruit of his intercourse with the stone, by the modeller ripped, as it were, gleaming from a womb. In a certain imitation of the more facile process, the carver now becomes more precise in his aim, more naturalistic: the children he wants from the stone must comply more and more with his own image. His successors, however, will sooner or later dissipate the underlying style without which any form of naturalism is meaningless. But the naturalism may yet be pursued without a single real plastic or carving idea. The ideal nude ceases to have any but a pornographic interest, even perhaps for its perpetrator, whatever he may say or think——and a commercial interest, of course.

To turn once more to stone relief. Classical relief, I have said, rarely possesses superb carving value. The flattening of form, so congenial to the light and density of stone, is rarely marked. Flattening entails the use of some perspective where a scene is crowded with figures; and it was the character of classical architecture itself which ruled out any such treatment.[1] A Greek temple, in

[1] See *The Quattro Cento*, p. 88.

particular, was so entire an expression of limestone, that a relief could add nothing structurally; while, executed in perspective, it would have disturbed the limestone geometry of the planes. It was as if architecture almost completely absorbed, and then restricted, carving aim. In some other countries, a more developed relief has still been part of the architecture without so marked a subservience. The other extreme is attained by some Indian temples in which structural conception might appear to be sacrificed to what is called ornamental carving: a misnomer; for the carving has not been conceived as distinct from the structure. It is the structure.

That will not appeal to modern taste which tends to deny, in any circumstances, a paramount sculptural value to relief. One is told that Renaissance relief is merely pictorial, merely bad painting. I trust the foregoing pages have put the boot upon the other leg; though I do not wish to suggest that a painting is inferior because it can be referred to a carving or plastic conception. If it were so, there would be no good pictures at all.

One is also told that a sculptural piece must be satisfactory from every angle; it must be entire, significant from in front, behind, on top, beneath and so on; whereas relief, of course, in worse cases than a picture, has only a front. Now the reliefs I am about to champion are to be seen from the sides as well as from the front. This has escaped everybody's notice, and it is the central point of their quality. But they have no backs. Behind them, and part of them, are slabs fitted to columns. Yet is this not to have a back? For myself, the entire piece of carving, even a primitive flint, is not the quintessential carving though it be the primary one. The carved stone that you take in your hand, that you turn over to examine every loveliness, has a created entirety which in the last resort I would rather associate with modelling. For the essence of stone is its power to symbolize objectivity. It should stand, be more or less immovable: and what better occasion for vital objectivity than when carving gives the expression to masonry itself, when relief shows the surface of the stone alive? Not often does it take this role. Quattro Cento carving, though, is of this kind, of which Agostino was the greatest master. Let me, then, if I am to convince you, define his mastery in detail, first pausing to consider the low relief that he inherited.

A few pages back I described how all the major values of stone could be glorified by the flattening and thinning of form in very low relief; how stone may thus reveal rounded forms that are yet altogether one with the matrix and with the building. Flattened shapes in relief, shapes that give *some* suggestion of the figure in the round, and consequently afford *some* value to a side-view, are common enough in Byzantine, Romanesque and Gothic relief. Except, however, in some Byzantine and late Gothic pieces, the flattening is not far developed, nor could it be further developed without proper perspective. But it is a mistake to regard perspective science as something altogether unequivocal, as clearly demarcating its users from their predecessors. Wherever on flat or flattened surfaces there is a suggestion of the round, there is use of perspective of some sort. Here again is the connection between the layer-like or flattened forms natural to stone, and pictorial art in general. For the widest possible definition of a picture must be the use of flat pigment entailing some suggestion of two or more surfaces. Should pigment be used without any suggestion of a variety of surfaces, it may achieve pattern, but not painting. Painting realizes on a single plane the tones of marble surfaces. Indeed, the very same sense of round shapes that are yet flattened out, which I find proper to stone relief, is sometimes to be obtained from Byzantine pictorial art; for instance, from the compressed attitude of the mosaic sitting Virgin of San Appollinare Nuovo at Ravenna. She is, in part, represented slightly sideways so that she shall the better appear to sit. As for one of the attendant Magi, his bending knees (that enable a large part of the haunch to appear), his twisting trunk, immediately put one in mind of the attitudes Agostino used in so many of the Tempio reliefs, by which he could suggest figures in the round. Again, the Byzantine terra-cotta reliefs in the Baptistery of the Orthodox are to be connected with Agostino's works.[1]

Thus, when perspective science was discovered at the beginning of the 15th century, it was the answer to an intensified acquaintance with stone. The Mediterranean limestone values came uppermost; and, of course, in a novel form, in a Gothic form after a thousand years or so of Christianity. But as usual the carving situation was bound up with the plastic. Given a new attention to

[1] The probability of direct influence upon Agostino on the part of such Byzantine work at Ravenna will be discussed in the next volume.

stone that dates from the proto-Renaissance, it was not irregular that the enormous strides in technique and perspective should have been immediately contingent upon a new aim in the more facile process, modelling.

Limestone, as I have said, marble in particular, possesses a soft light. Yet it is solid and durable. Its beauty is this fusion of the virtues of hard materials and soft materials. Nay, further, the purer marble is hard and brittle, yet owing to its metamorphic, homogeneous structure, is carved by strong tools with some facility. And it is probably due also to this character of marble, that modelling, the more facile process of homogeneous soft materials, has made in Mediterranean countries an unparalleled, continuous, intrusion into the carving of stone. Some intrusion of modelling facility heightens the 'human' limestone character, as we shall see in the work of Agostino whose art reveals a combination of plastic skill with a searching respect and love for the stone.

But the majority of Florentine Renaissance sculptors had no such continuous love. Already before the 'stone rush'[1] Florentine modelling was far developed, and it was the Florentines who upon the advent of the 'stone rush' gave the new command and the new conception to the rest of Italy. In my first volume I have described this phase and its connection, so far as architecture and

[1] One of the most obvious features of 15th-century Italy—and it is noted as such by contemporary travellers—was the crop of new stone buildings, and the investment of existent brick buildings with stone.

Carving, Modelling and Agostino

architectural decoration were concerned, with the dull Florentine sandstone, *pietra morta*.[1]

They loved stone little in Florence. The more typical Florentines answered to the spirit of the times, but not specifically. Their interest in carving too closely corresponded with their interest in the degree of modelling that stone could absorb. They made use of the deepened interest in stone a trifle ungenerously. Theirs was the poise, the equipoise, the cold purity of modelling conception. When I come to Florence from the Adriatic coast, I notice this at once—everywhere this poise of the bronze upon the pedestal. I have a sense of *Plastik*, I notice the prominent yet noble stomachs of the statuary, moulded, it is evident, not by eating but from outside by the sculptors. I admire the size of things, I admire greatly the poise of the open loggias and the great eaves that are like wings of wheeling aeroplanes along the streets. How they sail and wheel like the swallows who nest in them! Stately, naturally stately become the figures in the narrowness below, figures once fitted in voluminous robes and locks upon high heads. As I gaze at the planes of the eaves fixed in complicated rhythm along the Via dei Bardi, high over the straight, gloomy walls, I remember Verrocchio's bronze St. Thomas with a foot balanced without the niche on Or San Michele, I feel his calm locks and pointed face and the nobleness of his cloak. The noise of the Via dei Calzaioli, reverberating among the close grey stones, prevents this nobleness from gloominess and pride: and so it must

[1] More usually called *pietra serena*. Cf. *The Quattro Cento*, Part II, chap. i.

Carving, Modelling and Agostino

have always been in Florence; always the plastic assurance amid turmoil.

The evidence in Florence of any essential carving is less direct.[1] It exists in the works catalogued as Quattro Cento in my first volume (the connection with fantasies of stone exuberance there described makes them Quattro Cento), but it exists only in the large, and by no means specifically. The specific forms are the fruit of modelling, and are often enough realized in plastic materials. However, in the cutting of architectural decoration, sculptors sometimes showed less carving conception than in designs achieved with bronze or terracotta.

Perspective was developed by the Florentines, but was never the basis of their art. As I showed repeatedly in my first volume, the Florentine sculptors and the painters who derived from them 'used' perspective. They cared little for gradations in layers or in tone, except so far as they assisted naturalism. In carving as in modelling they realized the most realistic perspective without any intense gradation between adjacent surfaces. The foreground figures of Ghiberti's bronze reliefs are really free-standing, while the background figures are no more than outlined. Open the bronze gates or approach them from the side, and the reliefs will be meaningless, the foreground figures will be hor-

[1] On the other hand, the evidence that modelling had been put on its mettle, so to speak, by the augmented appeal of stone, is direct enough. The prevalence at this time of relief modelling in clay and terra-cotta must be referred directly to the influence of stone. Also, in these moulded reliefs, as in the stone reliefs, a marked flattening of form is usual, particularly of heads.

rible and precarious bits of pointed metal. In this connection I feel in sympathy with the modern criticism
of relief, especially relief on doors that presumably open
and shut. But such is not the relief I hail as carving.

Since they aped in stone the extreme naturalism of
Ghiberti's modelling, the Florentine cutters developed
an unequalled facileness. Sometimes they anticipated
the Baroque translation into stone of an extreme
Baroque modelling, as when the Rossellinos hung their
flying angels on the walls. These distressing figures,
which claim the poise of the hollow bronze although
they are ostensibly marble relief, preserve their positions
by being composed in reality of marble pieces that lie
close on the wall surface and that are secured by a
projection that passes within the wall. But there existed
relief carving in Florence, exquisite relief carving, even
though largely inspired by Ghiberti's plastic elegance.
Desiderio could not have thus carved the swags on the
Marsuppini tomb unless he had loved the marble. Yet,
if we compare him with Agostino, Desiderio is a modeller, conceives as a modeller. And the same is true
of Donatello. When Desiderio or Donatello carved a
Madonna and child relief, they composed it boldly, in
masses. And so, whatever the delicacy of the carving,
there is little, or no, *vital* connection between one surface
and the one immediately next to it. The child, although
he is the front surface, will be extremely flattened, so
that in composition he becomes of a mass, a plastic mass,
with the mother. There are cases when a significant
relation between one surface and an adjoining surface
is not so much unimportant from the point of view of the

general composition, as definitely undesirable. Thus the flattened top of a Virgin's head or nimbus is resolved into a rim cut away from the background. The centrality, the emphasis upon organized mass, require the rim to be divorced from the background, so that composition be the more definite, the more precise. Such a rim, however, is contradictory when seen from the side. For, the cutting away now appears as something so blatant and emphasized as to become a main feature, a positive denial of a nexus with the background, with the matrix. In brief, there is little care of stone surfaces as valuable and related in themselves.

Lombard cutters are even more at fault. Very often the whole heads of their crowded reliefs are cut away to an almost spear-like sharpness, apparent even from the front. It is only fair to say that of the carvers who worked principally in Florence, Desiderio is to be blamed least in this connection. He is considerably nearer to Agostino than were the Rossellinos and Majanos, or than was Donatello himself. Desiderio worked marble with a sensitiveness unrivalled in Florence. But he too seems a modeller by the side of Agostino.

Stone gradations are multiplied by an Agostino Madonna and child relief. Graduated surfaces are the logic of its form. Each surface sponsors a fresh disclosure. What is in front (the child) is less flattened than what is behind (the Virgin). The effects of actual difference in the depth of surfaces are not diminished as by Desiderio or Donatello in favour of a plastic mass, but emphasized with perspective. Thus the forms carved on the inner layers are progressively flattened. The further into the

Plate 7. Pietà: Donatello (London, Victoria and Albert Museum).

Plate 8. Madonna and child with angels: Agostino di
Duccio (London, Victoria and Albert Museum).

stone the more pronounced becomes the flattening of shapes: yet the inner and background shapes suggest no less contour than the outer shapes; with the result that they are luminous even in the dimmest light, as if their contours were indeed the face of the stone-block itself. So great is the contour expressed by these gradual or flattened interrelated surfaces that,unlike the reliefs discussed above, an Agostino relief will bear examination from the side.

This is the test of relief carving. If every surface is rounded into the next so that, seen from the side, the values of forms in the round are still composed there as a face to the stone, then it is the finest relief carving. The Florentine sculptors, one and all, had little use for perspective beyond a certain point. Agostino exalted perspective, so that every gradation of the marble's slow luminous face was given life by his hands. His low relief and its background possess a vital and vibrating concomitance.

Such general statements produce small conviction. Let us compare Agostino's Virgin and child relief in the Victoria and Albert Museum (Pl. 8) with the famous Donatello entombment (Pl. 7) that hangs on the next case, the one nearer the door. I have little doubt as to which of these two pieces the reader will prefer in photograph. For the greater the modelling conception in sculpture, the less are the values lost in photograph. The photograph of the Donatello relief gives you its point most happily. The design, the organization of masses, the elements of weight and stress and strain are clearly understood. The virtues of the Agostino relief, on the other hand, the gradual rounded cutting, the closely related equal tones and half tones, the luminosity, in part are lost. This Victoria and Albert Museum photograph is an exceptionally good one; yet the plate suffers by comparison with that of the Donatello. As for my other reproductions of Agostino's work, those plates which look the most striking are of the pieces that exhibit a more dominant plastic conception, such as the *David* and *Hercules* (Pls. 17 and 19).

But the disparity is not merely a question of photograph. The same judgment is likely to be made in front of the reliefs themselves. For contemporary educated taste is a good deal more academic in temper than one might suppose from all the talk and would-be 'modernist' profession. Now, academic taste only feels at home with plastic conception in the widest sense. That is one of the reasons why academic sponsorship of the classic is so woeful, so doomed. Like the pseudo-modernists, academic taste can only fully recognize design alone, albeit of a different sort, but equally the plastic sort. Be it modernist or academic or whatever else, the simple, swift or 'masterly' *organization* of masses is characteristic of modelling, be it oil paint that is slickly splashed about or Le Corbusier's lightning concrete.[1] Naturally, the Florentines with their power of organization, with their complete preconception (all the values of a Florentine relief can be suggested by a

[1] I am not denying the relevance to-day of Le Corbusier's building. I but make the point that his conceptions are purely plastic. At the end of this chapter I shall point out what difference this new (and inevitable) plasticity of building makes to the carving-modelling situation.

sketch), are continually acclaimed unrivalled masters among the 15th-century sculptors. At a moderate estimate only one out of a hundred trained admirers of visual art is as sensitive to the deeper philosophies of space and tone or carving, as he is to poise and rhythm or to the plastic side of composition. The majority will fully recognize the creative verve only when it has *fashioned* something out of formlessness. They see the shape and the other attributes of a primitive flint tool, but they do not see with the same absorbed attention that it is a flint. In a word, the majority are not highly sensitive to stone. They love texture and colour of course. They know this picture has good colour and that bad colour. But there it is, just colour or colourfulness: which indeed it is when employed for plastic conception. To them the concentrated use of tone necessarily means an impressionist effect. When will they see that tone is put to more uses in a picture by Piero della Francesca than in a picture by Renoir; when will a painter come forward who is incapable of conceiving this horrible idea, colour?

I, at any rate, put in a word for carving. And, indeed, there are signs that the original carving conception is to-day rediscovered. Already there are painters who disdain the moulding properties of oil paint, who, so to speak, prefer to polish and scratch their canvases like the carver his stone. An attitude of such kind—rather than the often concomitant abstraction in design—is the basis of the painting we feel to be contemporary.

I do not desire to minimize the appeal of the Donatello

relief (Pl. 7), though I am not averse from anticipating its photographic advantage. Its beauty is monumental. Nothing that Agostino carved was monumental. Hence his comparative neglect by the critics. There is nothing monumental about the nature of marble. But I will not deny that the effect of the Donatello piece, in common with many other plastically conceived pieces, is enhanced by the fact that it is carved in marble. And, of course, in such carving, some of the Renaissance general love for stone obtains expression. But this relief in no way qualifies as one of Donatello's Quattro Cento works; unlike, in this respect, the reliefs on the base of the Judith, which, although bronze, display the tense animation and exuberance that was primarily imputed by that age to flowering stone surface. Or, if you prefer, such humanistic eruption was imputed to all materials. But I have argued sufficiently that stone has a preeminent objectivity for which a flowering is most desired. It is the concrete thing, the sculptor's ideal object.

Here is, then, in the Donatello relief, the modeller's organization of masses realized in marble. The Christ's body is everything. Even in photograph you can follow the modelling of his stomach which is made 'anatomical' in the mode that is common to Florentine sculpture of this period. On the other hand, the further wing of the foreground angel on the right is no more than sketched in. *As surfaces*, the figures traced in the background, the background heads and the nimbi, have no aesthetic relation whatsoever with the masses in front. These background shapes are relevant only to the composition as a

Plate 9. History.

Plate 10. Rhetoric.

whole, that is, as shapes; which is not enough relationship for carving conception. But apart from the background shapes, in foreground, too, there is shown small feeling for changes in surface as significant in themselves. To Donatello, changes of surface meant little more than light and shade, chiaroscuro, the instruments of plastic organization. The bottom of the angels' robes is gouged and undercut so as to provide a contrast to the open planes of Christ's nude torso. The layers of the stone are treated wholesale. Though some of the cutting is beautiful in itself, the relief betrays a wilful, preconceived, manner of approach. In brief, the composition is not so much founded upon the interrelationship of adjoining surfaces, as upon the broader principles of chiaroscuro. Stress and strain is the point: anatomy, the then unrivalled plastic subject, is the point.

There exists a tendency for composition to be thus broadly organized whenever the sculptor has made a design and delegated to assistants most, if not all, the heavy slow work of cutting the stone. Here again we see a reason, this time an unattractive one, for the interpolation in carving of plastic values. The prevalent monumental aim of European carving has, at times, entailed the gentleman sculptor of manifold commissions, who draws sometimes, and sometimes models in clay. Several recent academic sculptors are reputed not to have handled a chisel in their lives, nor any other carving instrument except at meal times. Three-feet models of war memorials—a wet day's work—have been posted to Italy to be executed there in tractable marbles by subservient masons with the mechanical aid of pointing.

Carving, Modelling and Agostino

No wonder, then, that with few exceptions, the handful of serious sculptors who exist to-day concentrate upon carving and perform every stroke of their own work; no wonder they feel that they rediscover the very art of sculpture.

In the Renaissance, of course, there were hundreds of men who cut stone superbly. The most intense feeling for stone was abroad. Nevertheless, plastic conception lent itself to delegation of work, to its organization on a large scale. We see why Florentine aesthetic was so well developed, why the workshops were so big and efficient. In plastic art, at any rate, production breeds production. A plastic conception executed by able assistants does not suffer to anything like the same extent as a carving conception. The plastic conception already exists in the master's drawing. But the values of an Agostino relief, other than those of its plasticity, were achieved only in the actual carving process. Agostino's assistants in the Tempio often let him down badly; and it was inevitable that they should. One might say that the attainment of a carving conception cannot be delegated or hurried. But those peoples whose fantasies rely largely on stone, insist upon a multiplicity of statues. Thus, we realize once more that the very love for stone, for stone sculpture, entails the development of a plastic approach. For only with the aid of this approach can good sculpture become quickly extensive. And we see that when the tendency has run its course, when the original demand for stone is exhausted, a meaningless plastic sculpture, committed to academic design, remains.

Carving, Modelling and Agostino

We need, however, make no excuses for the cutting of this Agostino Madonna and child low relief. It is obviously by his hand.

The most marked difference between the Agostino and the Donatello (Pls. 8 and 7) is the former's effect of steady disclosure, in direct contrast with the latter's alternating light and shade. There is always the element of disclosure in true carving. Yet, contrasted with the Donatello, Agostino's intensely low relief at first sight may seem ribbed and fretted, fussy. You miss Donatello's bold plasticity. But then you cannot realize in photograph the subtlety of surfaces that preserve the marble as wholly marble. You feel a lack of rhythm. But why always seek for rhythm in visual art, why desire that rhythm or music and other temporal abstractions be conveyed by objects; why desire from the concrete an effect of alternation, since the very process of time can be expressed, without intermittence, as the vital steadiness of a world of space, as a rhythm whose parts are laid out as something simultaneous, and which thus ceases to be rhythmical? Rhythm, surely, is not so proper to visual art as immediacy; there is, surely, a certain priority of carving over plastic conception. Plasticity or rhythm in architecture and sculpture of the South has always retained some pronounced immediacy of effect through the dramatic presentation of feeling. In the visual arts of North and East, on the other hand, rhythm too frequently impairs spatial significance: too often those arts in essence are a visual kind of music. And how few appreciators of visual art understand anything about art, except about music and literature!

Carving, Modelling and Agostino

Agostino's tonalities elude you. You cannot, for example, realize from the photograph the effect of the apparently straight, if ridged, surface of the Virgin's undergarment that appears beneath her left hand. Carved, not modelled, are the carefully flattened heads, slow in roundness, yet so great in roundness that they will 'read' from an angle. Should you go to the Victoria and Albert, contrast in this respect the two Florentine reliefs, one on each side of the Agostino. They are absurd when viewed from an angle, when you see them as you stand in front of the Agostino. The poignancy of his shapes is not so much in themselves, as in their relations with his other shapes. This relationship is a much tighter one than in modelling. There is a poignant beauty in the triangular shape beneath the Virgin's wrist, inside her cuff. This shape is nothing in itself: for carving conception bestows an immense content and power on what, by itself, would be the most insignificant of forms. Notice the impassable little space between the Virgin's cheek and the child's head. It has the meaning, the shapefulness, of the intervals between forms in Piero's paintings. Such irremediable position between objects, shapes that are thus so far determined by their intervals, do not lend themselves, after a certain point, to the bold organization of masses that we admire in the Donatello. And why 'bold'? Because such plastic organization runs counter to the purely spatial conception of which stone is the symbol.

Yet, I will not deny that Agostino himself is an off-spring of Florentine modelling as I have defined it; that unless he had learned his trade in the Florentine

Carving, Modelling and Agostino

school,[1] he could never have developed so facile and flowering a technique, nor attained such naturalism; that some of the Florentine modelling clichés remained with him. But I have already admitted a constant interrelation between what I have called modelling and what I have called carving. I admire the infusion of such modelling into such carving so long as it enhances the layer formation of the stone. Further, I am willing to champion any marble piece, however 'modelled' its forms, where there still exists some wide reverence for stone, some evidence

[1] Agostino was born and trained in Florence. As a young man, accused falsely of theft, he sought his fortune on the other side of Italy. At the age of forty-five (1463), after completing his work at Perugia and at Rimini, he returned to Florence to find that the individual style that he had developed was not appreciated there. He could not attract any big commissions; though he was set to carve two colossi to be skied somewhere on the Duomo! In the end he returned to Perugia. It is a thousand pities that he, the master of low relief, was so often set to carve statues, quite apart from colossi. His later Perugian carving is for the most part lost: from the fragments it appears that in his public commissions his style was often ruined by the needed adjustment to contemporary taste. The earlier tabernacle in the Ognissanti at Florence is a lovely work: but the necessary homage there paid (a homage that entails a modification of Agostino's style) to the reigning Rossellino type of beauty is indeed pitiable. On the other hand, the lovely Porta San Pietro at Perugia, which belongs to his last Perugian period, shows how faithful Agostino remained to the Tempio; and so do the Madonna and child reliefs. As a rule, Agostino's statues are rather formal and exceedingly thinned, though far more frontal in conception than his best reliefs. Cf. the fragments now in the picture gallery at Perugia. One will conclude, however, that Agostino's peculiar genius for carving could have been sustained at its height only if he could have worked continually for such a man as Sigismondo. As we shall see, the very requirements of the Tempio sculpture coincided with his own bent.

or remembrance of stone culture such as the Mediterranean limestone culture. I give these Florentine plastic
stone statues and reliefs preference, as carving, over
much northern cutting that may have a minimum of
direct plastic aim but which, none the less, pulsates
with rhythm. Northerners have never loved stone deep
down; and no other material directs the fantasy to pure
non-rhythmic space.

This conception, non-rhythmic space, is difficult to define more closely: so let me again apply its sense to one
detail of the reliefs before us. Whereas in the Donatello
relief the angel's face on the Christ's arm is a most definite (and plastic) transition, on the left of the Agostino relief we see one face, as it were, causing other faces.
The essence of the carving, and of truly spatial, non-
rhythmic approach in general, is the juxtaposition of
similar tones, of related contours, of intrinsically related
forms. Every part is on some equality with every other
part, an organization that is foreign to the come-and-
go of rhythm. Work of this intensely spatial kind recalls
a panorama contemplated in an equal light by which
objects of different dimensions and textures, of different
beauty and of different emotional appeal, whatever
their distance, are seen with more or less the same distinctness, so that one senses the uniform dominion of an
uninterrupted space. The intervals between objects have
assumed a markedly irreversible aspect: there it all is, so
completely set out in space that one cannot entertain a
single afterthought. In visual art, the idea of forms however different, as answering to some cogent, common,
continuous, dominion that enforces the bonds between

those forms in spite of their manifold contrasts, gives rise to the distinctive non-plastic aim: and this idea was inspired, above all, by the equality of light on stone, an equality that dramatizes every tonal value. In Piero della Francesca's painting, by the religious reverence for spatial intervals, by tonal and perspective organization, all feeling, all movement, all rhythm, all plasticity itself, was translated equally into panorama terms. His pictures express the metaphysics of space or colour or tone. They are free of 'atmosphere', psychological or physical, as they are of anything emphatic.

See once more how shape causes shape in the Agostino relief (Pl. 8). The Virgin's arm lies tight to her diaphragm. There is the impression of a surface growing inward. This helps out the slight indication of the breasts. In the Donatello, an angel's hand is put flat on the Christ's body. It directs attention to the torso: it is a *general* tactile reminder. One obtains from the Donatello none of the sense of surface making surface to flower. Agostino was the master of undulation in the stone. His stone becomes a hotbed of shape. See the angel's head at the bottom of the relief, his hand clinging to the frame as if he had emerged from the back layers and had passed through the Virgin to the front, or as if the stone were a sea in which he rocked by his hand to and from a breakwater. Also, notice the poignancy of the child's curving shoulder juxtaposed upon the face of an angel behind, from which the shoulder's roundness graduates. Face and shoulder give each other shape. This is an excellent example of Agostino's use of tone, or, perhaps in the case of actual untinted carving, one should just call

it surface juxtaposition.[1] At any rate, compare this surface transition with the deep shadow around the shoulder and arm of the angel on the left of the Donatello
relief. There are no such gross and plastic shadows in
Agostino's carving. His placing of a shoulder against
a cheek behind, similar contours without a shadow between, remind one of Piero della Francesca's yet greater
juxtapositions of similar tones, unaided by the actual
changes of surface that facilitate this feat in carving.
Piero delighted to display his extreme virtuosity in the
employment of tone by using a practically identical
colour for something portrayed far behind, juxtaposed
to something portrayed well in the foreground. So complete his skill and so essential is it to his conception of
painting, so completely is that conception realized, that
with a fair amount of intelligence one might look at his
Flagellation at Urbino every day for a year, without
noticing in the picture a very astounding instance of
that feat.

This is the painting that presumes light, a more or
less equal light, another word for space as a homogeneous medium, in which all things are set out. Piero
could turn transition and movement into the finality of
such space. Lights, on the other hand, *lighting effects*, or
an emphasis upon chiaroscuro, these are to be connected with rhythm or poise, not primarily with stone.
Northern European and Northern Asiatic painters have
generally conceived light as the agency of atmospheric

[1] The reader will be able to discover for himself in my photograph many other instances of such mutually enhancing juxtaposition. An obvious example is the hair of the two angels on the
right.

Carving, Modelling and Agostino

effects: when left to themselves they have been, of all pictorial artists, the least connected with stone, the furthest committed to modelling conception. Such is the case of many sculptors, too, who have avoided the introduction of specific modelling shape and idea. This avoidance has availed them little, whatever strength and superficial purity, whatever profound absence of vulgarity, their more puritan temper has evolved.

Piero's and Agostino's conception depends upon an almost hieratic use of perspective. In terms of perspective was the religion of equal light, of space, of stone, expressed in that time. Anyone may experience this finality who is familiar with the air of southern lands. It is not because of marked difference in tone or in distinctiveness that you perceive this wall to be behind this wall. The bricks of the farther house-wall are just as clear, just the same colour. Each object stands in order, reduced to a common relationship by a common medium. You are aware of space: every process seems exposed as objects, all of them all at once in their degrees. More especially, just as the sun has gone down after a hot day, things stand. A luminous whiteness, as yet untrammelled by the dizzy approach of night, is common to sea, to road, to house. Stone gleams, the dust is white: what is of dark hue is dark, what is darker is blacker without mitigation. The sun has disappeared suddenly leaving the world arranged. After the long dazzle of the day, your eyes see the world exposed by a neutral medium which is but the fresh, caressing air. The evening stirs: the concrete world stands concrete. What was the passage of the sun has turned into space, and all that is left of passage are the invisible airs. Otherwise every phase, all subjective conditions, appear to have been transformed into objects arranged in neutral unbroken perspective.

It is when thus light or space imposes so uniform a dominion on objects that difference in tones seems uniquely real and poignant. There is nothing atmospheric about them. The relationship between objects becomes the essential part of their shape; and this their relationship is of tone and of perspective. Light marble pre-eminently, in most of its conditions and in most lights however dim or however violent, enjoys this tonal condition, since the equal light on stone tends but to mark its shape.

Once more I am back to the subject of Agostino. I have previously mentioned the tonal qualities of his cutting. I must now say more about his uses of perspective. Although much of Piero's finality in spatial exposition may be traced in his art, Agostino was also concerned in showing movement as a ferment on the surface of the stone. For both purposes he used exaggerated perspective: since both the tonal relationships and the ferment proper to his stone could be dramatized only by gradual curves, that is to say, by the flattened or perspective treatment of form. To describe exhaustively the method of its employment by Agostino would need a volume to itself, entailing an intensive technical study for which I am not equipped. I can but indicate a few general principles, remark a few details, a few characteristics of his carving.

In the first place, to show developed perspective in

Carving, Modelling and Agostino

carving, it is necessary to carve relief. Having argued a connection between perspective and stone, I now bring it forward to recommend the low relief, or at any rate, Agostino's relief in which the perspective cult is celebrated. Renaissance relief perspective is based on the same conical projection as painting perspective, with the difference that painting is projection on one plane, low relief on at least two planes: thus the latter's perspective is complicated by the thickness of those planes. Also, since the joining of actual surfaces must not be obscured by the use of perspective; on the contrary, should thereby be magnified, less simplification is desirable than in the case of picture perspective. High relief does not suffer this complexity to the same degree, yet has the difficulty in crowded scenes of one figure obscuring another, especially as seen from an angle. But those sculptors who loved, rather than employed, perspective, as far as possible avoided crowd scenes of the type that can only be treated in high relief, or in some combination of high and low. Agostino's best work is of low-relief single figures which manifest clearly the flattening he employs, and its integral connection with the block.

As I have often remarked, for such degree of flattening, perspective was essential. It is almost as if his figures were conceived in the round and were then pressed into low relief, so great is the roundness that is intimated by his care of stone surfaces. His perspective tricks dramatize to the full the propensities of stone: and since form in the round is there squashed out, the whole of that form is to be grasped from any angle. In sculpture, such

Carving, Modelling and Agostino

immediacy can be attained only by relief; and I think no one except Agostino has managed it, and he by no means invariably. Not more than twenty pieces or so in the Tempio Malatestiano are first-rate, one or two reliefs by his hand at Perugia, and the Madonna and child reliefs, the one at Florence, the other at the Victoria and Albert. We do not know how much else of the same sort has disappeared.

The ovoid is the perspective appearance of the sphere. The ovoid is the flattened sphere. Hence the ovoid, the thinned sphere, is the prevailing shape in Agostino's work. As he needs must work with ovoids, he began to visualize everything in terms of that form. Throughout his work he has given us this key. Thus, for instance, when he represented clouds, they are cut to pure ovoidal shapes (Pls. 2, 3, 12, 30, 44, 46, 48). Fingers, of course, and fish were dear to him. So too, globular hair-locks and the elongated contour of breast or stomach, buttock or thigh, beneath tight strands of transparent drapery. Such transparency, again, affirmed the slight translucence of the marble. He also used drapery to enshroud the whole figure and reduce it to his dominant shape. *History* and *Rhetoric* in the Tempio are oval forms (Pls. 9 and 10).

Agostino had various ways of enforcing perspective. Most forms in his reliefs have a perspective of their own apart from their contribution to the general perspective. Occasionally this individual perspective is in opposition to the more general one, but, at the same time, the former thereby makes the latter poignant. Still, the particular, and sometimes even contradictory, perspective of details, while it yet must fit in and help to make the design, also puts emphasis upon graduation of surface and neutralizes a simple modelling assessment of general masses. This perspective treatment is not peculiar to Agostino's work. To some degree it appears in all Quattro Cento carved and modelled relief. In all representation, of course, there is the tendency to show the lower half of an object or figure as seen from above, and the higher half as seen from below. Such a mixture of perspective is common everywhere. It is the most simple means of showing more of the object or figure than would a strictly eye-level representation.

But see to what extent and to what resultant shape Agostino employed this principle. Let us turn once more to the Madonna and child relief (Pl. 8). The general principle obtains for the relief as a whole. At the top, the head of the Virgin is inclined slightly downward and to the left, as she looks at the child. Her face we see from below; but since she tilts her head downward we see well above her forehead, we see her hair, veil, crown and nimbus on the back of her head. (The edge of the nimbus is bevelled inwards so as to bring it forward.) We see two-thirds of her head owing to perspective flattening. We would see even more of her head if it were not turned to the side as well as inclined downward. The right side of her face is shown as far as the further edge of the eye. This right side is so flattened that in actual dimension it is only half as long as the distance from the nose to the further edge of her left eye. The ear is shown in complete profile, the angle at which an ear is most significant. It is a complicated ear,

Carving, Modelling and Agostino

in rapport with the shell forms of the niche behind. The child's face is seen definitely from below, whereas the angels' heads adjoining, and those on the other side of the relief, are on eye-level. Moreover, whereas we see the child's face from below, *we see the top of his head and even parts of the back of it from above.* Otherwise, so much of the head could not be represented. This transition from one perspective to another passes muster because the head is tilted to the side and downwards, while the eyes look slightly up. Yet the perspective is even more complicated than this. Parts of the face we see on eye-level, and the ear, like the ear of the Virgin, is represented in complete profile.

At the bottom of the relief, the child's right foot, foreshortened on the outward-tilted framework, is seen entirely from above in accordance with the general perspective.[1] Yet we can see slightly underneath his left foot. Also contradicting the general perspective, though at the same time reflecting its plan on a small scale, the tilted angel's face whose chin abuts on the bottom frame is seen on eye-level, if not from below; while the top of his head, like the top of the child's head, is seen from above. The perspective of the vase on the right is also independent of the relief's general perspective. The vase's base is seen from above, its middle on eye-level, its lip from below. Such was the usual way of treating vases and candelabra in Quattro Cento arabesques.

These various perspectives cohere: in this manner

[1] That is to say, the general perspective of the bottom half of a composition as represented from above, the top half from below. Cf. p. 151.

Plate 11. Relief of an angel: Agostino di Duccio (Perugia, San Bernardino).

Plate 12. Relief of angels: Agostino di Duccio (Perugia, San Bernardino).

Carving, Modelling and Agostino

several aspects of an object were represented, while individual perspective, so far as it was the microcosm of the general perspective, emphasized that general perspective, that sense of many aspects. To some degree you will find such treatment in all Quattro Cento work, whether it be stone, bronze or terra-cotta, and in all work that approximates to being Quattro Cento. And this helps out a classification of Quattro Cento sculpture in terms of technique. *Wherever you find relief forms, be they ornament or figure, arabesque or swag, wherever you find these shapes, whatever their position, turning to show to you their maximum, like flowers that thrust and open their faces to the sun, wherever that is the salient point about them, then that sculpture is Quattro Cento as I define it.* Decoration sculpted with that feeling will never look 'stuck on'. For hand in hand with vertical perspective goes horizontal perspective, the flattening which means gradual and rounded shapes that issue from the block. Of such flattening, Agostino was the supreme master.

Consider the child of the Virgin and child piece (Pl. 8), consider how much of his body is shown by this low relief. You say it is like painting. This, as criticism, means nothing to me. For I can here see and touch all the values I love in stone. Painting is an offshoot of such carving. The Egyptians sometimes carved the legs and head in profile, the rest of the body as frontal. Agostino's figures are a softer stone development of the Egyptian aim. A characteristic attitude, of which the child is an example, is a sideways bending of one or both knees, thus bringing in the curve of a buttock; or an arm thrown across the body bringing in the shoulder and even the shoulder blade. The first attitude (Pls. 2, 12, 13 and many others) requires one leg in rounded profile, so that one sees almost the whole calf, while the other leg, represented frontally, is, when the cutting has been crude, so flattened as to appear without a shin bone. Furthermore, the bending knees cause the part of the legs between knees and thighs to be represented at a receding angle that is easily foreshortened; which, in turn, enhances the circular and ovular swirls, represented on eye-level, around the stomach and the hips. The trunk is often bent slightly forward over the knees, while the shoulders and head turn slightly the other way. This attitude entails a nodal vortex about the stomach and around the hips, out from which the rest of the figure undulates. Such figures appear to float rather than stand. The effect is increased by swirling hair and swirling drapery that now conceal, now disclose, limbs and breasts.

These figures appear to be embedded in some buoyant white liquid such as mercury. The soft yellowish and luminous Greek stone was cut by Agostino to show its original liquidity and condensation. The bodies of the floaters are thus enmeshed and carried, but their heads float higher and rest upon the buoyant surface (Pl. 11). From the knees to the navel, there is a swirl, a vortex, in the typical Agostino figure. This tends to endow the males also with the female contours and the female suction. Looking at the relief of Diana (Pls. 13 and 44) and of the other planets, and particularly the one that represents the spring tides under the aegis of Diana (Pl. 48), one feels the vast seductive influence of the

Plate 13. Diana.

Plate 14. The Crab over Rimini.

moon. Not till the last words of this volume shall I have set out to my own satisfaction this lunar mythology and all that it means. I must show Isotta as the moon, and Sigismondo who built the Tempio as her counterpart. For directly, even more, indirectly, the Tempio celebrates Sigismondo Malatesta's love for Isotta.

The floating image must now give place to another. Agostino's figures inhabit every plane of the waters. If they float near the top, they also lie upon the bottom whence they seem to pierce each ripple as it passes. The Tempio is at Rimini on the Adriatic coast. Ripples come low and in quick succession upon that beach in summer. On arriving last June, I walked to the end of a small jetty. A white-enamelled iron chair stood upon the sea-bed. From the jetty I clearly saw it standing in the depth, with its round back elongated to an oval or shuddered to an ellipse. What indeed was its shape? But there it stood. I thought at once of Agostino's sculpture in the Tempio, of those flattened forms in which an influence was at work. In general it was a water influence. The reliefs were marble and dry; but they were luminous: and thereupon I felt the whole deep connection of limestone and water.

Next day in the Tempio I saw the Mediterranean countries as water and water-life congealed into stone: I saw the elements in flux and trees growing from a crested marble wave. *Venus* (Pl. 6) is represented as coming to land in a chariot drawn by two white swans. Around her legs and piled up behind her are the waters. The topmost wave is smooth, without a ripple. It is the shapely mountain side. On one summit there grows a myrtle tree, the aromatic evergreen shrub of limestone soil. The rose flowers in a valley of intermediate swell.

The relief of the influxion of the moon shows land peaks and similar trees encompassed by the flood (Pl. 48). The trees are tinted black in both reliefs. They are the dark evergreens of the Mediterranean light, trees that flourish from the limestone whence by temple or on promontory they show off the pure sculpture of marble. A youth rides the buoyant flood in a boat. But should Diana's mingling influence relax, his boat would be left high and dry on the back of a whale or sea-dragon. For half the seas have attained the same degree of solidity as have the mountains of liquescence. The creation of further limestone is in hand. The influence at work keeps the flood encompassing the shores to which an elephant comes in alarm.

Such pregnant waters, such trees, such pyramidal peaks beneath the ovular clouds, figure also in the relief of the *Crab* (Pl. 14). Rimini, the Adriatic and the hinterland are again represented. The limestone layers are the waters. Notice the river Marecchia flowing between the hills and out into the Adriatic. It is the rainy, the torrential flow. In such waters *Aquarius* or Ganymede stands (Pl. 46). They flow behind him from the ovular clouds that muffle his left arm. Clouds, like so many torpedoes, hide *Mercury's* knees (Pl. 45), and upon his head is the pyramid as a pontifical mitre. From his knees to his navel and again about his head there is a vortex. It is the whirring night from which *Diana* emerges clean (Pl. 13). It wraps the loins of the *Twins* (Pl. 47), sucks evil *Saturn* (Pl. 15), hurls up the dripping

Plate 15. Saturn.

Plate 16. The Virgin.

Virgin (Pl. 16), encircles the *Dance* (Pl. 36) and distributes her wiry coils of hair. But the predominant vortex is about the hips. These swirling eye-level middles that disclose so many attitudes and so many surfaces, tend to put 'out of drawing' the upper part of a figure's trunk. But three lovely reliefs at Perugia show best how profound is the style based upon this mannerism (Pls. 3, 11, 12). Agostino gave back to marble its primeval eddies. This vortex is sometimes recalled and set to work by the incision of a few curving lines in the background (Pls. 2, 5, 13, 16, 44).

Where no vortex appears in the middle of a relief, the idea of it yet lingers. In the relief of the influxion of the moon (Pl. 48), this centre, represented on a level with the eye, is the first big pyramid with the tree in front of it. Hence a further poignancy. To the pyramid, to the new limestone accruing from the waters and their life, is attributed the concentrated powers of the whirlpool whose beauty, now that it is a smooth stone, may be shown by a thin and gradual shape in complete objectivity. Here is expressed in unconscious parable the whole appeal of limestone, the whole underlying mythology of Mediterranean art.

Finally, in the matter of stone and water, I refer again to the shape of fish, to their extreme yet rounded flattening, to the predominance of the oval form. No wonder the representation of marine life has always delighted the Mediterranean limestone carvers. But it was only in Quattro Cento carving that marine decoratives, principally in the shape of dolphins, attained a paramount exuberance. There is nothing stylized and ornamental

Carving, Modelling and Agostino

about Quattro Cento dolphins or sea-centaurs or scor-
pions. Yet fish are the fundamental carving shape. Fish
slither and wriggle in Quattro Cento relief and arabesque. The stone is alive with them. Putti, with the marble
dust in their eyes, ride the dolphins (Pls. 1 and 35); a
fluke is sometimes cut clear from the background. The
block itself wells over larger deep-sea forms within.
Shells encrust the architectural members. They are not
stuck on: they cling; but also they flower there, bloom
there: they are also stone-blossom. For the water and
the water-life from which the marble was formed, in
their stone shapes symbolize also the cliff, the earth, its
flower and its fruit. Such shells express the first geological concretion in the history of the marble, serve to
symbolize the later fruitfulness of the soil which covered
it from the skies. Thus sea and land, upon whose intercourse Mediterranean civilization has depended, were
celebrated as one in the marble. Either as land or as
sea-fruit are the shells and acorns. In the last analysis,
stone-blossom and incrustation are different aspects of
the same principle. Marble, then, was the prime instrument of Humanism. For such fantasies as found their
home in marble were humanistic fantasies. Therein
was implicit the friendliness to man, the 'natural' un-
strained exuberance which treats of elemental nature
with so little anxiety in proportion to its dynamic
strength. The tension is all of life: from death is bor-
rowed but its objectivity, its unmitigated petrifaction.

It may seem that I use the sculpture of Agostino to
further a set of ideas. I have written of particular work

Plate 17. Section of a door jamb: David.

Plate 18. Section of a door jamb: Gideon.

Carving, Modelling and Agostino

by him in relation to chosen photographs. Like a doctor with a nervous patient, I have avoided bringing to the reader's notice realities which might dampen his ardour. It is full time to make some reference to the actual condition of Agostino's work in the Tempio.

The Tempio was never finished, and most of what exists of the original work was done in a hurry and under difficult circumstances, as I shall relate in the next volume. Agostino was the master sculptor in the Tempio: by no means all the reliefs were the work of his own hand. We know the names of his numerous workmen, but nothing about their respective skill. Few of the reliefs have the degree of finish possessed by the Madonna and child in the Victoria and Albert Museum; and it will be obvious that skill in actual execution is far more important to a carving design, as has been said, than to a modelling design in which, however unfinished or rough, the 'idea' may well be apparent in full force. On many reliefs in the Tempio the marks of the claw are distinguishable. In some figures, the very subtle flattening technique, as executed by assistants, has been grossly simplified. (But when one has grasped Agostino's carving 'idea', so much more difficult to understand than a modelling 'idea', one does not mind.) Perhaps the body of a figure has been flattened successfully, but the floating head, for which prominence was desired, has been treated crudely with higher, too much higher, relief.[1] Some reliefs were partly coloured and have now lost their tints, or have since been badly treated with modern colours. The first chapel to the left has been ruined by a

[1] Cf. Pl. 46.

modern attempt to restore it in 15th-century style. The draughtsmanship of nearly all the reliefs is, as one would expect, by no means eminent: but in many cases, too many cases, it is definitely inadequate.

Still, for those who are sensitive to stone, I do not exaggerate the Tempio's revelation. As for others, I believe that many faults they find in the internal architecture as well as in its sculpture, reflect both such people's obliviousness to carving, and their search for the modelling upon which their aesthetic values are based. Plate 17 will have many admirers. It is lovely, but not so much as carving. It is a plastic figure. These powerful furrows possess the rapid Donatellesque organization. *Gideon* (Pl. 18), on the other hand, is lovely as carving. His nakedness has a gradual yet revelatory virtue that comes of its flattening, at one with the block and with his immense shield whose edge is rounded. The conception of *Hercules* (Pl. 19) is midway between that of *David* (Pl. 17) and that of *Gideon*. *Hercules* is beautifully flattened: we can see round the calf of his further leg. But the upper part of his body is 'constructed' on the emphatic principle, so is his girdle with its deep furrows. *David* is the most modelled relief in the Tempio, if we except some of the very inferior infant games and shield-bearer reliefs to the second chapels on the right and left. We shall not look for Agostino's execution among any of these.

On the other hand, it is interesting to note that Agostino was a very fine modeller in the specific sense of the word. For instance, the coloured plaster relief by him in the Bargello at Florence (Pl. 20) is a superb piece of

Plate 19. Section of a door jamb: Hercules.

Plate 20. Plaster relief of Madonna and child with angels: Agostino di Duccio (Florence, Bargello).

modelling. Here are the swift or loose organization of masses, the deep shadows.[1] He understood the large-scale treatment also, a plastic treatment that was soon to develop into the Baroque, a style still further removed from carving conception. This clay Madonna and child relief is as purely modelled as the Victoria and Albert piece is carved.

In Quattro Cento carving, plastic aim, however strong, is yet subservient to the love of stone; an ideal situation for the cutting of medium hard stones, marbles and sandstones. In the case of hard stones, modelling skill is most likely to be altogether out of place. Their obdurate hardness has never served as so broad a repository for the elastic images of men. However, the cutting of hard stones is better appreciated in this age. The hard stones' resistance to plastic aim saves it from being entirely judged by the usual modelling standards. Sensitiveness to carving goes as far as that. But medium hard-stone sculpture, when it contains an evident plastic infusion, particularly 15th-century marble, is less fortunate; since it is judged entirely in terms of plastic qualities which do not reflect its deeper character.

To one important aspect of Agostino's carving I have made little reference, since no photograph can illustrate it. I refer to the subtle undulation in his reliefs of their backgrounds. One may say that as a rule the block tends to be less cut away at its top and at its bottom. In many of the Tempio reliefs, as well as by heads that are in higher relief than bodies, this tendency is ex-

[1] Notice the absence of complicated perspective or of subtlety in surface juxtapositions.

panded by the bottom-most sections being of still higher relief and serving as ground for the figures (Pls. 11, 16, 18, 19, 21, 23, 47). All Agostino's subtlety was used on some of these pedestals, on their shapes and curves and sections. They help to show how deep the block has been cut. Occasionally they are rounded to the sphere or ovoid so that the feet shall the better slope for us to see on top of them (Pls. 9, 10, 22).[1] Sometimes the pedestal is used to represent rocks, with a few flowers incised on their barrenness whence grows an aromatic tree. *Mars'* scythed chariot descends a precipice (Pl. 23). But it is in no great danger. A hurricane blows it back, blows back his ovular shield, pins it to the block, hurls back his cloak and the tree on which his eagle has perched. Mars himself gleams; and the wolf, whose hide seems mail-clad hard, is unruffled by the wind.

Capricorn (Pl. 5), of the full ovoid udders, reaches up a peak to nibble the mountain oak. She balances upon the naked stone. See how it is cut to fundamental stone shapes, to gradual curves and smooth ripples; not gouged, not furrowed.

Mars' chariot is seen from above, *Venus'* chariot from more or less the eye-level (Pl. 6): but *Diana's* chariot is seen from below (Pl. 13). Water and fishes gush out beneath it. The horses which draw the chariot, however, are represented on eye-level. Diana herself with the rinded moon in her hand is represented from below.

---

[1] The base of the Madonna and child's outward-tilted framework serves a similar function, as we have seen. It is an integral part of this carving.

Plate 21. Music.

Plate 22. Philosophy.

Carving, Modelling and Agostino

The background is tinted dark. Owing to the mixture of perspectives, Diana is given a dazzling height above us. She is truly in the sky, above the clouds at her horses' feet. She steers above us straight out of an enormous night. At the same time, due to the flattening[1] of shape performed with the porridge-coloured Greek[2] marble, she is a luminous figure, she is the moon herself.

The *Diana* relief is the bottom one of the pier, the *Venus* the top one (Pl. 24). *Yet Diana's chariot we see so much from below, while Venus' chariot is represented on eye level.* This curious mingling of the heights and the depths has the magnetic quality of moonlight, moonlight of the luminous, brown shadow, moonlight which can cause even the mountains to appear like ridges in the basin of a waterless sea.

And so, under the aegis of the moon, goddess of waters and fish, goddess with the luminous marble face, I take leave of Agostino for the present.

This chapter is finished; but a postscript seems inevitable.

The fine arts are rooted in the handicrafts, the handicrafts in various manual labour whose vastly traditional character, to put it mildly, is changing. Of what kind, if any, is to be the new skill, the new handicraft? I have no intention of pursuing the subject. Instead, I call attention to one contemporary change which is simple

[1] Cf. the not altogether satisfactory treatment of the horses' knees so that they won't jut out.

[2] In *The Quattro Cento* I said this marble came from Verona. I am now almost certain that it is a Greek marble.

enough, but which in itself upsets the whole balance between carving and modelling.

I have defended the low relief by pointing to its direct connection with masonry, with stone architecture. Hitherto, stone or otherwise, all developed sculpture has been founded on an association, at least, with architecture; if not specifically with buildings, then with monuments, shrines, tombs and so on. Except in the case of fetishes and other small personal objects, architecture and sculpture have in every stone-using civilization gone hand in hand: or, rather, sculpture has been dependent upon building. This connection mirrors the pre-eminence that stone has enjoyed as the desired building and carving material, has ensured the preservation of some possible carving values amid the usual growth and eventual dominance of modelling conceptions. But to-day stone is no longer the desirable building material. What is more, *modern building materials are essentially plastic.* These materials have little emblem of their own. With an armature of steel, Le Corbusier can make you a room of any shape you like. He can express speed with a building. Rooms will be fashioned. Their organization will be simple sheer design that has no use for trappings, least of all for sculpture.

Everywhere the slower carving processes are superseded. Manufacture, modelling, has superseded its fellow. Such, we have seen, was always the European trend, though it was sustained, paradoxically enough, partly as a result of the great ambitions of European peoples in carving processes.[1] Synthetic materials take

[1] Cf. p. 123.

Plate 23. Mars.

Plate 24. Venus, Mercury and Diana, three reliefs on entrance to the third chapel on the right.

the place of age-old products in which fantasy is deposited. The majority of our pavements and of our new buildings are made of synthetic stone; not merely concrete, but synthetic stone that can be fashioned to almost any effect that is desired! You need to know something about stone to distinguish it from this moulded product. Modern scientific power of synthesis fashions a fundamentally new and plastic environment.

Stone architecture is prolonged but a moment by synthetic stone. Stone architecture dies, the mother of the European visual arts for more than two thousand years. In Europe of the historical period, brick and mud and clay and wood construction never superseded stone. They had their individual life; still they were largely substitutes for stone. At any rate European men have always built with stone when they could afford it and obtain it. But to-day stone architecture is dying. The creations of Le Corbusier and others show that building will no longer serve as the mother art of stone, no longer as the source at which carving or spatial conception renews its strength. Architecture in that sense of the word, indeed in the most fundamental sense of the word, will cease to exist. Building becomes a plastic activity pure and simple: whereas, in the past, building with stone or its equivalents has not been (at best) a moulding of shape with stone, so much as an order imposed on blocks from which there results an exaltation of the spatial character of stone.

Mountains and pebbles still exist: but so far as stone loses its use as a constructive material, it loses also power over the imagination. Civilized man is surrounded by

Carving, Modelling and Agostino

natural objects the intensity of whose imaginative import will continue to diminish.

What future is there for carving, or for the full spatial conception?[1] I have remarked that the strength of such modern painting as is truly contemporary is founded upon a reaction from modelling values in favour of carving values. But should the growth of plasticity, of manufacture, in labour and in art, overpower carving activities altogether, there is then no future for visual art as hitherto conceived by the European races.

[1] Should the reader still be puzzled by the all-important equation of 'carving values' with the 'full spatial conception', he is advised to turn back for a moment to pages 144 and 145 particularly.

Part Three

Stone, Water and Stars

Chapter Five

The Tempio: First Visit

Rimini is not an attractive town. There are the sands and the Adriatic, flat hotels and villas stretching half a mile from the shore with hardly a stop. But these are cut off from the town by the dirty, jagged knife of the railway. You are then in a town of cobblestones, in no way picturesque; a country-town that sprawls almost in the northern manner of industrial suburbs. What abruptness abounds is harsh and without colour. The port where the river Marecchia flows into the sea beside the bathing establishments, the Roman bridge over the Marecchia, the Roman arch on the Flaminian road, these are points of interest; but as centres of departure and as points of reference in the mind, they do not 'work'. The streets, of no great length, seem endless as the Commercial Road. For whither could they lead? Not back to any great distance in the past in spite of the superb Roman bridge and the Roman arch, in spite of the Rubicon which was one of the streams just north of the Marecchia and of Rimini. The Rubicon served as boundary between Roman Italy and Cisalpine Gaul. But Rimini has lost the keen air of a frontier town, and if you were expecting some link

The Tempio: First Visit

with Julius Caesar, you will in your disillusionment find
the other extreme; you will find the sprawling country-
town (neither on the sea nor off it) to be made up of
dull and hopeless interiors, innocent of aspidistra, but
all the more *triste* for that, because bare and cold in
winter; inevitably the retreats of *Risorgimento* memories
and other comfortless yet Italian Victoriana. You will
not, it is true, see the same old man every day, but each
day different old men who exhibit a certain unnecessary
presence of mind: can they not (they are thinking),
should they want to, take the tram up to the beach, up
to the Romagnol Lido that is hacked by the gales of
winter? So the depression diffused by the more indifferent deadness of other nearby towns, Pesaro or Fano
or Cesena or Forli, where the hotels are enormous provincial palaces converted into chambermaidless tombs
that lie over noisy streets, is more impressive. There, the
gloom of heaping roofs and bolted and unbolted wooden
blinds may well shatter you.

But it would seem that the spirit of Rimini is diffused
and scattered, over-harried by shunting and important
trains, just because that same spirit stands isolated,
though conserved, in the silent stone of one building.
Noises pass away from it. And if you would liquefy all
the energy, all the life both of the town and of the district, all the life that here stands concentrated in stone,
if you want a Gothic and even Roman Rimini, you must
follow the fantasies and the noisy researches of these
pages, each of them stimulated by contemplation of the
one building, the Tempio Malatestiano. Perhaps my
task seems an unnecessary one. Perhaps you have seen,

The Tempio: First Visit

or you will be able to see, the building for yourself. At any rate here are some photographs. And for my part, why should it be worth my while to transpose into terms of drama what is immediate and objective to the eye? At best, I shall be creating in an inferior art, inferior in objective realization, working many impressions that could be obtained in five minutes at Rimini. Certainly, though I have studied the subject on and off for six years, I have added no new intensity of feeling to my first 'ignorant' impression of the Tempio. I have only found images and names and explanations and reasons and theories—in general, literary data—to express what on July 5th, 1925, I knew at once of the life, the landscape, the condition of which the Tempio is the emblem. My excuse must be that the potential content to be gathered from looking at the Tempio will be understood by the majority of cultured people, or even noticed by them, only when someone has done his best to transpose that same so objective content into images and ideas: and then, not into poetry pure and simple. There must be a good deal of explanation as well.

So, as heretofore, I shall take the reader step by step. Each cadence and each break will be a transposition into rhythm of what these stones mean, each fact and each idea will correspond to a carved emblem; and the literary form, with its self-conscious come-and-go, with protagonists and drama, must emulate the white certainty of Alberti's encasement.

On that first visit to Rimini I knew little of Sigismondo Malatesta who built the Tempio, beyond the name. It is easy enough for me to give you at the outset the whole of my knowledge of that time. I need but copy out a paragraph or two of Baedeker (1909) as follows:

"*Rimini*, pleasantly situated about ½M. from the Adriatic at the mouth of the *Marecchia* and the *Ausa* (the ancient *Aprusa*), with 29,545 inhab. and extensive fisheries and silk-manufactures, is frequented by Italians and Hungarians for its sea-bathing. A fine avenue of plane trees leads from the Porta Marina (see below) to the beach. The shifting sands are apt to obstruct the harbour.

"*Rimini*, the ancient *Ariminum*, a town of the Umbrians, became a Roman colony in 268 B.C., and was the frontier fortress of Italy in the direction of Gaul, and the termination of the *Via Flaminia*. The town was extended and embellished by Julius Caesar and Augustus. During the Exarchate it was the northernmost of the 'Five Maritime Cities' (Pentapolis *Maritima*), which were ruled over by one governor. The other four were Pesaro, Fano, Senigallia, and Ancona. In 260 Ariminum became an episcopal see, and in 359 a council against Arianism was held there. The town afterwards belonged to the Longobards.

"In the course of the 13th cent. the Malatesta made themselves masters of the city. In 1288 Giovanni lo Sciancato ('the lame'), surnamed also Gianciotto, put to death his wife, Francesca Polenta of Ravenna, and his brother, Paolo il Bello (an event from which Dante derived the episode of 'Francesca da Rimini' in the 5th canto of the Inferno, and Leigh Hunt the materials for his 'Story of Rimini'). During the following century this family ruled the greater part of the Romagna, and also, for a time, the mark of Ancona. Under Louis the Bavarian they became viceregents of the emperor, but Cardinal Albornoz afterwards succeeded in reducing them under the power of the pope. The Malatesta family, divided into the Pesaro and the Rimini branches, distinguished themselves as condottieri, but also as patrons of learning. The most famous scion was *Sigismondo*, son of Pandolfo (1417-68), who united the gifts of a great military leader with the most violent passions. He attracted painters and scholars to his court, in order to secure immortality for himself and his mistress (afterwards his wife), the clever *Isotta*.—In 1528 the people revolted against the Malatesta and placed themselves under the authority of the pope.

"A broad road leads from the *Station* to the Porta Marina, within which it is called Via Umberto Primo. After 4 min. we follow the Via del Tempio dei Malatesta to the left, passing a dilapidated Renaissance palazzo.

"**San Francesco** (*Duomo, Tempio dei Malatesta*), originally a Gothic edifice of the 13th cent., was magnificently remodelled in the Renaissance style in 1446-55[1] by Sigismondo Malatesta from designs by *Leon Battista Alberti* and under the superintendence of *Matteo de' Pasti*. The windows of the original building are retained.[2] Of the façade unfortunately the lower part only has been completed, while the dome intended by Alberti to surmount the choir is wanting. The choir itself was restored in 1709. On the plinth are the initials and arms (the elephant and rose) of Sigismondo and

---

[1] This, and the subsequent figures, refer to the note I append to Baedeker's account (on p. 175).

The Tempio: First Visit

Isotta, who were to have been buried in the arcades on either side of the portal (see below).

"The vaults of the S. side contain the sarcophagi of poets and scholars whom Sigismondo entertained at his court. In the first four are the remains of *Basinio* of Parma and *Giusto de' Conti*, the poets; *Gemistus Pletho* (died 1451),[3] a Greek philosopher whose corpse Sigismondo brought hither from his campaigns in Greece; and *Roberto Valturio*[4] (d. 1489), the learned engineer. In the others repose several physicians and a bishop of the 16th century.

"INTERIOR. To the right of the entrance is the *Tomb of Sigismondo* (d. 1468). Most of the plastic ornamentation of the chapels was executed by *Agostino di Duccio* of Florence. FIRST CHAPEL on the right: above the altar, St. Sigismund of Burgundy, patron-saint of the founder; by the pillars, allegorical figures of the virtues. SECOND CHAPEL OF THE RELICS (Santuario; closed), containing a (restored) Fresco by *Piero della Francesca* (p. 62; '*Petri de Burgo opus 1451*') Sigismondo Malatesta kneeling before his patron St. Sigismund, with the castle built by him on the right.—In the CAPELLA DI SAN MICHELE the 3rd to the right, is the *Tomb of Isotta* (d. 1470),[5] on the left, erected as early as 1450, with the motto 'tempus loquendi, tempus tacendi' at the top. The archangel on the altar by *Ciuffagni*,[6] is a portrait of Isotta. By the pillars, angelic musicians.—FOURTH CHAPEL on the right: by the pillars, the planets and other fantastic representations from a poem by Sigismondo[7] in honour of his mistress.—FOURTH CHAPEL on the left: by the pillars, allegorical figures of the sciences.—THIRD CHAPEL on

174

The Tempio: First Visit

the left: Children's games, probably by *Simone di Nanni Ferrucci*,[8] a pupil of Donatello.—The FIRST CHAPEL on the left is named the Capella dell' Acqua from an ancient statue of the Madonna, represented as sending rain. On the left is a sarcophagus for the reception of the ancestors of the founder, with two reliefs, representing the House of Malatesta in the Temple of Minerva and the Triumph of Sigismondo. By the pillars, above the elephants, two portrait medallions of Sigismondo."*

* There are several minor errors in this account, and I suppose it is my duty to correct them in case an intending student should otherwise be misled. The inaccuracies are culled from the pages of Yriarte (though Baedeker has avoided many of Yriarte's errors, an astounding achievement in 1909), the Frenchman at whom the Italians have thrown too many bricks. For, though his inaccuracies, his reading of documents and his guesses, were wild, Yriarte sometimes hit the right note forcibly; as when he suggested that Agostino was chief sculptor in the Tempio (since proved by the inscription Ricci found), and when he attributed the Milan relief to Agostino (cf. p. 105 n). Yriarte's greatest coup was the publication of documents, relating to the Tempio, from the archives at Siena. These comprise Sigismondo's mail of December 1454 which was intercepted by the Sienese. Malatesta studies owe a great deal to Yriarte (*Un Condottiere au XVᵉ siècle*, Paris, 1882).

I merely tabulate the suggested corrections without giving my references: since a full account of them, and of their bases, would overburden what is intended merely as a precautionary note.

[1] 1447-1457 is a better date. Work also went on sporadically from 1457 till Sigismondo's ruin in 1461.

[2] This is extremely unlikely: though the matter is still disputed in certain quarters.

[3] Gemisthon Plethon died in 1450.

[4] Valturio died probably in 1475.

[5] The documents show that Isotta was living on 23rd March, 1474, and that she was dead by February 1475.

[6] It is unlikely that this is the work of Ciuffagni, nor is there anything to show that the statue is a portrait of Isotta.

[7] Alas, the poem is by someone else, nor has it any reference to the Tempio sculpture.

[8] There is nothing to support this, nor to suggest it.

The Tempio: First Visit

That is what I read in the train from Ravenna. I had heard, of course, that at Rimini there were to be found a fine example of early Renaissance architecture and some sculpture of the same date. I had stayed long enough in Venice to realize that the infinite love for stone by which it had been made so variously emblematic, was especially related to the art of the early Renaissance. As yet I had no knowledge of Florence. Florence was my ultimate goal in which, as it happened, I was to be almost bitterly disappointed. But meanwhile I could see the early Renaissance in Venice and near Venice. First I stopped at Ferrara, then at Ravenna to see the Byzantine churches and the mosaics. As it happened, the visit to Ravenna, from which I came direct to Rimini, was most fortunate. For thereby I was able at once to gather connections between the Byzantine achievement and the Tempio.[1]

On the way from the station at Rimini there is some fine 16th-century brick-work: San Girolamo. I found a custodian to open up the interior. On the ceiling of the choir there is 'St. Jerome in the Desert' by Guercino. "Who painted it?" I asked her. She was full of assurances, though taken aback. "Sigismondo, Sigismondo Pandolfo Malatesta;" and giving her worst idea an emphasis as is the way of some Italians, she repeated the name with impressive satisfaction. "And Isotta made the holy water basin?" About this she could not but agree as there seemed no alternative: though the marble was hardly a courtesan's material.

[1] The elucidation of this connection, and all other matters of historical analysis, are reserved for the next volume.

The Tempio: First Visit

Sigismondo and Isotta, I realized, were fixed ideas in people's minds; or were they just substitutes for Paolo and Francesca? But in any case my curiosity about the Tempio was increased. For it seemed unusual that stone memorials by themselves should feed popular romantic misconception: in comparison with poetry, that is; especially post-medieval building. Could it be the Tempio itself which was causing the Riminesi to evoke the names of Sigismondo and Isotta in an art encounter with foreign bathers? And I would have known—so I thought—the Sigismondo and Isotta story if it had been extensively 'written up'. What was the story, and did the stones speak? Surely there was no gesticulation, no eloquent statuary. And how did a more compact architecture suggest a story?

Here is the Tempio façade on the left (Pl. 25). I nearly passed it by; it is so compact. Nothing draws you: it is silent, without rhythm. It is steadfast like a blind face. The fact that it is unfinished starts not one single speculation. Do you wonder what expression the blind man had when he used to see? No: his face is complete as it is. This is no shrine, no temple, but a church; Gothic San Francesco upon which Alberti has built a classical encasement. You can see the brick of the old San Francesco above where the stone encasement is unfinished. That is the only modulation.

Stone is rare in these parts. Aemilia and Romagna are poor in stone. The Istrian of which the façade is built does not weather so well as that in Venice; it does not come from the best quarries.[1] But the blocks are

[1] Some of the blocks were lifted from the graveyard. Tomb inscriptions can be deciphered on the façade and flanks. Sigismondo

The Tempio: First Visit

strong and deep. How sudden are these dense white stones in the sprawling town! The encasement is tall, steep for its length. The proportions of the four three-quarter columns and of the blind arches between them upon the high stylobate are beautiful, strong, serene. The mouldings, delicate enough in composition, are so uncompromising in their certainty and relevance as to be ferocious—in the way that a mathematical conclusion drawn from a dense conclave of figures can be relentless yet sublime. Science and art, delicacy and strength, were never so close together as in the early Renaissance. The façade neither goes up, nor down, nor across. It stands white and strong. Nothing could be more four-square than the box-like imposts upon the stylobate, from which the columns rise. I would prefer to have avoided this word, 'rise', because of its directional meaning; though if I were describing a Greek temple I would use it willingly. But the Tempio façade is far too compact to afford any sense of directional emphasis. This compactness can only be gained by the ligature of arches and by avoiding at the same time their more usual effect of progression. It is true that the massive centrality of the door is emphasized (Pl. 26): one is aware that this façade is a very careful composition: and the setting-off point of all design, as we conceive it to-day, is some principle of centrality, its emphasis or avoidance. Yet the ratio between the shapes, between the oblong imposts, the depth of the stylobate ledge, the

was always hard up and always on the prowl for stone. He lifted some of the port of Rimini itself. His most extensive haul probably was the Istrian stone that had been intended for a new bridge over the Metaurus at Fano.

Plate 25. The façade. Designed by Alberti.

Plate 26. The entrance. Designed by Alberti.

blankness of the blind arcades, and the triangular depth
of the pediment, overcome the massive centrality in
favour of a general steadfastness. Whatever their design,
this is a characteristic of all Quattro Cento buildings.[1]
Their architects abhorred centrality, since it entails
progression from both ends of a building, as much as
they abhorred a decentralized rhythm. Yet they employed arches. Their conception of composition was
less plastic and infinitely more alive than ours. They
obtained their effects with classical forms yet without
academic manoeuvre, often without variations of any
kind. And in this context, Bernini, Sir Reginald Blom-
field and Le Corbusier are to be classed together in the
opposite camp. A modern architect may doubt whether
a building upon identical arches, with an identical
arcade above, without variation, without central feature, could possibly 'come off', far less afford the highest
sense of the steadfast. Let him look one day, if he will,
at the Procuratie Vecchie by Mauro Coducci in the
Piazza at Venice. And what is true of the horizontal
lay-out in Quattro Cento buildings is often true also of
the vertical. The Quattro Cento architects who built
with masonry were less prone than we to talk of 'good'
and 'bad' design (just like that), as if all aesthetic considerations could be reduced to the simplified mechan-
ism which an inevitable use of these adjectives suggests.
They were less concerned with plastic purity. They
wanted each stone to be beautiful: as far as possible they
avoided the situation in which one group of stones sur-
renders a more positive function in order to give em-

[1] But not so of Brunelleschi's unvaried arcades. See Vol. I, p. 106.

phasis to another group of stones. The Quattro Cento conception of proportion was without severity and without extravagance. If you take care of the material's significance, proportion will largely take care of itself. They achieved sublime proportion with the minimum of cunning and the maximum of feeling. The rather empty Vitruvian 'rules' were a good enough conscious aesthetic; for architects inspirited them. Again, sometimes the proportions are unsatisfactory and it does not seem to matter much.

All architecture deserving the name possesses *some* carving, as opposed to a plastic, significance of this kind. It is, at root, the character imputed to limestone itself which has immortalized the employment of classical members in architecture. Only thus, from the angle of the material's fitness and liveliness, rather than from the more conscious angle of pure design, does proportion in architecture attain sublimity. And since, to-morrow, if not to-day, building becomes in all respects a purely plastic art, it will less confuse the values of this art if we find another name for it, foregoing the term architecture altogether.

So much for the plan—a better word nowadays than design—of the Tempio façade. On the flanks there are deep bays, portentous as an aqueduct (Pl. 4). The first five bays on the right side have a sarcophagus apiece. Behind are the brick walls and the Gothic windows of the interior.

As I look, the tense *cohesion* of the encasement impresses me so forcibly that already my mind has received the full stimulus that will need to find expression in such phrases as 'stone-blossom' and 'incrustation', suggesting an almost *organic* connection between architectural members and between background and ornament. This quality provides the fundamental difference from nearly all other architecture, and particularly from other buildings, be they Greek, Roman, Brunellesque, High-Renaissance, 'Classical', Baroque, Empire, or whatever else, that employ, entirely or in part, one of the classical orders. Employment of classical pillars or pilasters nearly always means an impression of distributed weight and coherence. But see how that impression is intensified on the Tempio façade into something far more dynamic, see how the pilasters are *grown* from the wall-space, grown steadfastly like a flower, without palpitation; see how incrusted is the effect of this most classical pediment within the central arch (Pl. 26). You can no longer distinguish architectural members. The thing is organic, one, everlasting.

In Ravenna I had seen something lasting, something complete and certain. The Byzantine mosaics, and to some extent the architecture too, possess a deep religious assurance. This art celebrates the triumph of Christianity and of statecraft. Certainty is so great, content so deep, that expostulation is not only unnecessary, but impossible to its style. Yet the Byzantine achievement pales before that of the Tempio façade. For we admire here, not the certainty of the objective world gained for religious or political concepts, but objectivity itself, stones themselves, which are celebrated and dramatized as a content rather than as the means to realize or express a content.

The Tempio: First Visit

As I stand before the Tempio, every tune falls away from my head. I encounter the stalwart face of the rose. Upon the broad stylobate there grows the Malatesta shield quartered with the monogram $. A massive wreath circles the shield, joined on either side to a tongue-like leaf of the Malatesta rose (Pl. 27). This shield and upright rose, with long and gripping leaf, alternate, except for the occasional interruption of an elephant or other emblem, in a zone of decoration along the façade and down both flanks. It is not a structural part of the design: but thus to call the shields and roses 'decoration' tends to obscure their quality, their quality of growth from the stone slabs. They exhibit the stone alive: and, indeed, the forms of the roses in particular and the technique of their carving are most unusual. I did not grasp at first how very conventionalized are their forms: the sense of exuberant naturalism they immediately convey, hides at first the actual simplification of their structure. Their four petals curve uniformly inward; from the stout stalk below, the leaves branch out.

No wonder I noticed first the exuberance of this growth: there is something almost monstrous about these turgid stalks! The Malatesta rose is a tropical growth in miniature, an immense trunk with huge subsidiary shoots such as would stifle a deserted town within a year. It belongs to the foraging kind of vegetation that is almost animal. These roses are on the stylobate at Sigismondo's behest, to provide a forest for his heraldic elephants and to support his shields.

The stalk or trunk of the rose shoots from a massive sheath whose fibres loop outward, and whose length

Plate 27. Rose and shield decoration on the stylobate.
Probably after the design of Matteo de' Pasti.

Plate 28. Base of pilaster to first chapel on the right. Architecture of Pasti: elephants probably after Agostino.

curls round to be a basis for the whole form. The sheath's end, however, curls up and divides into flukes or scrolls.

Now this stylized fantasy of the rose affords no effect of stiffness or of abstraction. Almost every shape is worked out to an effect of exuberant naturalism. Since the forms are not in any way copied from nature, it is as if the sculptor had invented a naturalism of his own, as if he lived in some world where these forms were natural. Whence springs the elephantine impregnation that distinguishes Sigismondo's emblems? The top and bottom of the 'I' in the $ monogram are fluked in the same manner as the root of the rose sheath. A connection between Isotta and the rose—that is, if 'I' stands for Isotta and 'S' for Sigismondo—suggests itself.

The Tempio had shut that first day, so I examined the outside carefully: and when later I was clothed with the patchy night of Rimini, my impression of the building dwindled (but with no relaxation of steadiness) to an image of one of the roses carved on the stylobate. This upstart flower was in dynamic relation with the masonry whose mouldings it overlapped. I was conscious in the 15th-century architecture and sculpture, of a tension to reveal itself, to make manifest. The forms in the stone put the structure at a tension similar to the most vibrant second of a singer's longest note. All is shown, put outward. I felt strongly the compulsion to make life no less objective than the stone into which all human passions were translated by this art.

During that night, lovely shapes grew upon the surface of my sleep as upon the stone. So next morning

The Tempio: First Visit

when I walked into the Tempio, I recognized the reliefs that are luminous in the dim light. I saw the tall and tempestuous Gothic chapels on either side of the nave as a dense, highly coloured, outburst that needed, for its fixture outside, encasement by Alberti's majestic white stone. My concern on entering was not as to the design of the interior (which cannot fill anyone with particular satisfaction), but as to the force of emblematic sculpture that demanded so casket-like an encasement. The flatness of this interior Gothic, high upon the walls of which diminutive yet squat pilasters flower, heightens the luminosity of the reliefs on the chapel piers. The wall-spaces are emblazoned with Sigismondo's $ and with the rose. Elephant trunks, as plumes to a casque, break out above Isotta's tomb (Pl. 37). $ is carved in balustrade (Pl. 32): shield bearers in the upper zone between the chapels and upon the entrance wall carry the mark upon their shields: everywhere the 'S' licks over and under the 'I' just as the rose-leaves embrace the shields upon the stylobate. There is elephantine foliage around the Gothic arches to the chapels: the predominant colours, blue and gold amid the stone hues, look personal and keen, interspersed in vault and spandrel above the porridge-coloured Greek marbles of the reliefs: everywhere there are coloured discs nailed to wall-fronts; centres of gravity like navels.

The first three chapels on either side are all that concern us:[1] for beyond the third chapels there is only

[1] In the description of the Tempio quoted from Baedeker (p. 173), *four* chapels of 15th-century construction are enumerated on either

Plate 29. Angel holding up canopy on wall of first
chapel to the right.

Plate 30. Angel holding up canopy on wall of first
chapel to the right.

The Tempio: First Visit

eighteenth-century adaptation. Each pier of the chapels has three lots of three oblong reliefs. One lot is on the outside plane, another on the inside, and the remaining one (Pl. 24) between the other two below the arches. At whatever angle you stand to these piers, you will see at least one, and probably two, zones of relief; and they will be catching the light differently. On the piers of the first chapels, relief is high: on the piers of the other chapels, relief is low. The reliefs of the third chapels were those which principally concerned us in Chapter IV and will concern us again. But let us now see as well some other aspects of the Tempio, many of which are to be connected with the name of Matteo de' Pasti.

My first impression, however, was of the luminous figures on the further pier of the third chapel on the right, the reliefs of Diana, Mercury and Venus (Pl. 24), though I had progressed but a few paces from the entrance.[1] But, before proceeding up the church, let us look in at this first chapel on the right, the sculptures on whose piers are nearly in the round. The piers are scooped out into niches to contain these figures (Pl. 31). At the bottom of each pier a box-like base, emblazoned with Sigismondo's emblems on its three sides (the fourth side of each pier and base joins the wall), rests square upon the nicely calculated black backs of twin basalt

side. In my description, no account is taken of Baedeker's second chapels since they are not visible from the aisle, being beyond the doors that I shall presently describe.

[1] The light in the Tempio is a Gothic light, that is to say, the rays come through Gothic windows behind the classical encasement. Hence one poignancy of the reappearing pagan figures that the faded barbaric light illumines.

elephants (Pl. 28). The weight that pours down their flanks and their close ears, causes their foreheads to be bulbous: but only their trunks that rest upon the plinth between their forelegs are notched and wrinkled to the strain.

I did not notice any bizarrerie in this architectural arrangement: for my impression was not of something exotic nor even profuse. On the contrary, reinforced no doubt by theatrical elements which might so easily have appeared Baroque and which emphatically did not, my impression was of tightness and compactness to a degree I had not known before. The stone, I felt again, shows everything upon its surface, steadfast like the open face of the rose.

Except that they denote this rare tension, the reliefs are not remarkable. Indeed, those of the prophets and sibyls on the piers of the opposite chapel are negligible.

In a sense, the design of the deeply cleft piers is 'bad' structurally; while the mingling of Gothic with classical mouldings upon the bases (Pl. 28) is clumsy and ill-adjusted. But does it matter at all, is it not part of the effect? See again the tension and steadfastness of this arrangement: see how the garlanded shield upon the square base curves like a flower to its fixity above the elephants' foreheads. The mouldings are no more monstrous than the florid Malatesta rose itself expressing a very personal myth we feel. See how tight is the fixture of the Virtues guarding their cavernous niches with which they are carved in a single piece (Pl. 31). The *singleness* of the exuberance, the alliance of surface and

Plate 31. Sculptured niche.

Plate 32. Balustrade. Probably designed by Pasti.

depth, are the means by which the tension to make manifest appears so solid.[1]

There are two very low relief, life-size, angels carved on each flanking wall inside the chapel (Pls. 2, 29, 30, 43). They support canopies held at their apex high up on the wall by angels of fuller relief. The low-relief figures are among the masterpieces of Agostino di Duccio. By distortion, by the use of drapery, from their attitudes, many aspects of sculpture in the round are achieved. Thus, no statue, no work cut free of a case of stone, nor even a higher relief, can emulate their quality of apparition.

The sense of fixture, obtained from the statuary on the piers and from the elephants below them, conjoined with the apparitions upon the walls, makes this first chapel an epitome of the Tempio's character (Pl. 31).[2]

I leave for last mention the chapel's balustrade (Pl. 32), since it summarizes all that has been said. Its qualities

---

[1] Similarly, the bronze fruit upon stone panniers that form the bases to the piers in the third chapel (Pls. 13 and 15) does not strike one as an insensitive vulgar extravagance, but rather as a dubious means of tension. The bronze is like a damson mess between the planes of bread that make a sandwich, and, like the jam, the thick bronze fruit bestows a continuous authority on the planes that seemingly squash it out above and below.

[2] In view of my aim to present the 'point' of the Tempio, I do not stop to remark that many of the Virtues and shield-bearers in this first chapel, and many other reliefs in the Tempio, are crudely conceived or crude and hurried in execution. Nor have I remarked that Agostino himself (it might be expected) was a mediocre and probably unwilling carver of statues. Such considerations, and an account of the Tempio's defacement by modern additions, can be left to others: in the case of many observers they will pretend that they see little else, although, at the same time, they will admit that

are of thickness, thick, replete, cornucopia, thick shields, thick round pieces, solid wheels of stone, broad and loud and smooth on their rims; and of apparition, the apparition of the peacock's spread tail, of finery notched and crusted, in fact of all associations with the shell form, loved by the Renaissance, a form here shown on its side encased by a half rim; one feels that the swags alone, bumping up between the round pieces, curb and fix their propensities to roll. The stout hand-rail of the balustrade and the course below press the round pieces between them with such violence that, since their roundness is not squeezed into an ellipse, we feel the more their solid strength whose thickness we can see. No doubt this is the work of Pasti. For Agostino invented a compression of such forms that made of them ovoid elongations. As do the shields, the round shapes, heaviest of coins, possess on their faces the low sculpture of emblems. And we pass within the chapel to see their other sides, as if they were upright struck coins, so rich and so heavy that, rather than turn them, we must walk round. Here again we see carved the upstart rose, poised upon the wheel like a winged monster that hovers taut and undarkened on the face of the early sun (Pl. 28). Here on

there exists some general romantic charm in this interior. Thus, critics are captivated by the Tempio, though, principally in view of the unrelieved standards of plasticity by which they judge sculpture, they cannot praise it overmuch.

The thorough pedestrian critique has been performed, notably by Corrado Ricci (*Il Tempio Malatestiano*, Bestetti e Tumminelli, Milan, 1925, 600 copies), to whose book I am profoundly indebted. I write now—and by no means exhaustively—of those features only which inspire my theme, and which, to my mind, are all-important and neglected beauties.

Plate 33.   Door to a chapel. Designed by Pasti.

Plate 34. Door to a chapel. Designed by Pasti.

The Tempio: First Visit

the next coin-like shape, an ancient Malatesta emblem,
the three heads.

Discs, rim within rim, characterize the jambs of the
square-framed doorway (Pl. 34) next to the first chapel,
and of the corresponding doorway opposite (Pl. 33).
In the moulding of the discs, in their adjustment to the
rectangularity of the whole design, in the reliefs on the
panels between the discs (Pls. 17, 18, 19), the latter door
is preferable. But it lacks the sculpture above the pediment of its fellow and also the coloured marbles[1] between the jambs and the rectangular frame: and it is
the other doorway, the entrance to the Cella delle Re-
liquie (Pl. 34), that is the lovelier of the two.

The modern purist may condemn this doorway for
the rather clumsy admixture in its design, of square,
oblongs and circles, among which the triangle of the
pediment and the forms contingent on the pediment's
boundaries are uncomfortably placed. But, of course,
judging from a photograph he cannot take into account
the colours of the marbles or the particular *brio* of the
carving which this cumbersome geometry serves to
enhance.[2] Current vulgarity, current lack of emotional

[1] These coloured marbles, together with those used above the
main portal and as discs on the façade, are probably some of the
stones that Sigismondo stole, or bribed the monks to let him take,
from the Byzantine church of San Appollinare in Classe near
Ravenna. In photograph the door without the dolphin reliefs
looks better as design than its fellow. Moreover, the absence in the
former of the mouldings on the inner side of the shields seems an
improvement. But what thus appear as structural defects in the
door with dolphins are actually the means of its superior colour
and an integral part of its Quattro Cento steadfast effect.

[2] The heavy tooth moulding of the rectangular frame loses its
effect of clumsy or undue constriction when the colours and tex-

coordination, have driven the purist to relish above all
else the indisputable shapes, the indisputable scaffold-
ing, around which all plastic conception has been built.
Nowadays, the scaffolds themselves are the only
aesthetically possible new buildings: their extreme no-
nonsense geometry provides some reassurance amid
emotional chaos. The purist, however, ignorant of carving values, is not free of a pronounced monotony in his
perceptions. Sensitive to draughtsmanship, insensitive
to the liveliness of stone, he cannot perceive the emotional content of these disc-like forms with their alternating convex and concave centres, a stone-blossom and
an incrustation between which the outward and inward
curving shield in the pediment holds the balance: the
same shield holds the balance also between the juxtaposed square and circular forms that our purist so
thoroughly dislikes.

When Pasti designed the doorway under the deep influence of his patron's *virtù* and with the whole unconscious surge of humanistic aim behind his art, knowingly
or unknowingly he had for his particular inspiration
Sigismondo's shield with the Malatesta chequers
quartered with the ₷. Sigismondo's valour in the field,
his pride in war, the very clanking of the battlefield,
shield on shield, boss against boss causing indentation,
the torn canopies on the great horses' backs held by
bossy buttons of gold, the approximation of real and
heraldic, of naturalism and of an invented naturalism to

tures are seen. Then one also sees that the light but cavernous
pediment has a powerful, almost Gothic, thrust that is kept steadfast and tense only by the outer moulding. The thin, reduplicated,
pediment lines are, as it were, the shrill cries the elephant contains.

Plate 35. Putto on dolphin over tympanum of a door.

Plate 36. The dance.

The Tempio: First Visit

express it—all these aims and impressions associated with the shield as an emblem and as an artistic motif are amplified and enhanced by Pasti's door. The model for such amplification was Sigismondo. Another sign of Sigismondo was the elephant; the elephant that amplifies his neighbourhood, trumpeting up the sky, trampling the earth, banging wide through thickets that gather rank behind him upon the murmurous grass.

The pediment has many deep rifts: upon them ride Agostino's miraculous dolphins, lashing up their tails on to the backs of the broad putti astride (Pls. 1, 35). They glisten in white marble (the doorway itself is of the porridge-coloured Greek), kept to a triangle by the great rectangle of tooth ornamentation which expresses an enlargement[1] of the chequered armorial upon the shield. The curving, inclined, elegance of this shield itself, its square and circular attributes, are enlarged by the close interplay, both tall and wide, of the squares and circles already remarked, and by their concave and convex mouldings. The mouldings that enclose the niches with their prophets are again an abstraction of the shield shape, being upright oblongs with their shorter lengths curving in and out respectively. The medallion that figures on the centre of the beam frames an elephantine *Fortezza* holding her two bits of broken column, two tusks found in the undergrowth.

Elsewhere the chequers and the rose. The trough-like mouldings around the discs with emblems on the jambs

[1] An extension, in turn, of the tooth moulding, characteristic of Venetian Gothic, appears in the treatment of the manes of Diana's horses (Pl. 44).

are an extension of the manner in which the $ has often
been carved in the Tempio, that is, with a trough in
the 'I' and similar segments in the 'S' which serpentine
where the letter curves under or over its fellow. This
licking 'S' has relation also to the leaves that bind the
shields and other emblems on the stylobate: the flukes
with which the 'I' is generally terminated top and bottom
—and sometimes the 'S' as well—are related to the
similar treatment of the rose's sheath and of the dolphins' tails. The steady face of the rose, in turn, has
many extensions: the stout garlands around the coloured
marble discs that lie between the jambs of the door and
the tooth frame; the garlands about the discs in the
spandrels of the façade, and many other garlands.

It is worth remarking the exact position of the discs
with trough-like mouldings on the jambs of this door:
the manner in which they replace the inner mouldings
of the jambs and the manner in which they meet the
transverse moulding (as in a latchkey); also the intervals
that the disc mouldings make with the ledge over the
beam. In original and spontaneous niceties such as these
there resides the flower-like and steadfast effect of
Quattro Cento carving.

The traveller should by now have grasped the main
trends of the Tempio's imagery. And so when he moves
along the right to the second chapel, the one with
Isotta's tomb, he should receive the full impact from
the blue and gold baldacchino and from the elephants'
heads upon the casque (Pl. 37). He should welcome
the chapel's balustrade (Pl. 38) with its columns in the
style of such Venetian bridges as the Ponte della Paglia.

Plate 37. Tomb of Isotta. Designed by Pasti.

Plate 38. Balustrade with putti. Designed by Pasti.

The Tempio: First Visit

In their symmetry and lighter hue, the small, stout pillars of transient porridge-colour may suggest to him the elephant's trunk. For these columns, and those of the corresponding balustrade to the chapel on the other side, are the only free-standing columns of the Tempio, inside or out; and the shape between column and rail may easily suggest the massy convergence by which the elephant's forehead lengthens into a proboscis. Moreover the seething grey surface of the rail above, in its deliberate broadness and generous angles receiving the light, suggests some smooth brain or switchboard that directs a dynamic force.

Upon the live rail putti are rooted. In each case putto and rail are the same block (Pl. 39). The putti are the only non-relief figures in the Tempio [1] with the exception of the enthroned San Sigismondo upon the altar of the first chapel, the archangel Michael upon the altar of the second chapel, and the shield-bearers at the base of the upper pilasters between the chapels. All these statues are only seen from the front. In fact they are far more frontal in conception than the reliefs. But the putti with their shields, at one with the rail, are designed for many angles of approach. When you pass inside the chapel you do not review a row of uniform behinds. For each putto has shot up differently from the smooth tumultuous stone; each presents his shield at a different angle. Wherever you go there will be some with their backs to you, seemingly convulsed; yet they will be turning their heads to see if you have seen, while

[1] I am not, of course, taking the additions of subsequent centuries into consideration.

they control or lean on their thick shields, although these are almost as big as themselves. The putti have a swollen vigour, an elephantine[1] lustiness. They are heavy, alert; they grew where their shields grew. A ribald precocity results from their oneness with the rail. They are never separated from their mother whom they ride and trample, each upon his block.

The shields have their emblems. One putto leans with all his weight on an outward tilted shield that is reversed, with the rose upon it upside down. At least one other mourns: and that should be their role. However gay in themselves, they are professional mourners. For here on the wall of the chapel depends Isotta's tomb weighted and supported by Sigismondo's elephants (Pl. 37). Above, two trunks wave the pedestrian motto 'Tempus loquendi, tempus tacendi'. The catafalque, furrowed like a monster's hide, discloses a sarcophagus on which three times is carved the magic date 1450. Underneath the slab a yet more magic date is recorded, the year 1446 in which Sigismondo first possessed Isotta.[2]

---

[1] Cf. a putto on the base of the left pier in the third chapel to the left. His feet are elephant's feet (Pl. 40).

[2] It was Ricci who in 1912 found under the bronze slab with the inscription: *D.Isottae. Ariminensi. B.M.Sacrum. MCCCCL.* a marble slab with the inscription: *Isote. Ariminensi. Forma. Et. Virtute. Italie. Decori. MCCCCXLVI.* Perhaps the first inscription had to be concealed as it might outrage the susceptibilities of some powerful person, probably the Pope. The 1450 inscription is repeated three times on the monument. Almost from the day of its unveiling discussion has raged as to whether the *D* stands for *Divae* or *Dominae*, Goddess or Mistress. Such equivocation is typical of the Tempio symbols. $ may mean several things, and was probably designed to do so, partly in case one meaning had to be denied occasionally. A few more deliberate experts, notably Soranzo, hold that $ refers

Plate 39. Balustrade rail with putto.

Plate 40. Pilaster plinth with putto.

The Tempio: First Visit

Time is jumbled about in the Tempio. Isotta's tomb was
built when she was young and alive: was built in no
mood of premonition, but to feign a triumph over death
by lifting the sarcophagus on to the backs of sage and
glorious monsters; and by delivering the funeral procession to the antics of eternal putti that stamp about
their mother's body; and by fixing everywhere the
steady rose. So in the reliefs upon the entrance piers,
putti pack the face of the stone, handling such closely
ordered instruments as harp and organ.

We have seen enough for a first visit: let us leave before the mental picture becomes blurred. That picture,
though, requires for its greater precision a few touches
that will convey the circumstances of Sigismondo's life.
While enduring these few pages we shall lean on the
brecciated rail of the balustrade to the next chapel,
since we may the more easily reflect there upon Sigismondo.

On the piers of this chapel are the planet reliefs[1] to
whose significance the subsequent chapter is devoted.

solely to the first two letters of Sigismondo's name. The date 1450,
inscribed altogether twelve times in the Tempio, was, like 1446, a
high-water mark year for Sigismondo. It was then that his position
in Italy was dramatized for him in the form of the honours be-
stowed by Pope Innocent V at Fabriano; and it was then that the
general reinvestment of San Francesco was conceived. For there
is no reason to think that the adornment of the first two chapels on
the right, which had been undertaken before this date, was in the
first place part of any larger scheme.

[1] More accurately described as reliefs of the sun, moon, five
planets, twelve signs of the zodiac and an influxion caused by the
moon. For brevity I shall continue to refer to them as the planet
reliefs.

The Tempio: First Visit

We lean on a perforated balustrade[1] of Verona marble, a Quattro Cento masterpiece (Pl. 41). Below us are the generous rubbed forms that the uncertain substance of this marble makes essential,[2] and to which, in any case, its glowing hues incite. The twin elephant heads serve as the epitome of that massy growth we have attributed to the Malatesta rose and other emblems. Around the trunks curls a blunt scroll with the motto 'Tempus loquendi, tempus tacendi', a time for the elephant's shrill assertion, a time for the elephant's weighted secrecy. His genius for instant revelation inspires all Sigismondo's emblems. We take his motto as our text.

Sigismondo was an aristocrat and a condottiere or soldier of fortune by profession, as had been so many previous Malatesta. A dominant aspect of his life is clearly mirrored by the disadvantage under which one so proud of his family started, and by the greed and craftiness of his original enemies. Sigismondo was illegitimate. His father, Pandolfo Malatesta, died when he was ten. The two next years Sigismondo spent at the Rimini court of his uncle, Carlo Malatesta. Both the father and the uncle were famous condottieri and men of culture. Carlo died. The Papacy was closing in on those lands that the Malatesta had held as papal vicariates for two centuries. All through the 15th century the popes were designing to recover the direct tenure of this and other fiefs in Umbria, in the Marches and in Romagna. At the beginning of the 16th century Cesare Borgia

[1] The chapel opposite with the reliefs of the Arts and Sciences has a similar balustrade.

[2] See *The Quattro Cento*, pp. 73 and 74.

brought the policy to a successful conclusion, and the families of Montefeltro, Malatesta, Manfredi, Ordelaffi and Baglioni, to name but a few, were sooner or later deprived.

Without parents, with traitorous advisers, Sigismondo was fighting to hold Rimini at the age of thirteen. His brother Galeotto who ruled at Rimini on the death of their uncle was a religious maniac: so on his own initiative Sigismondo saved the capital of the Malatesta dominion, already divided between several branches of the family. Galeotto died. Rimini became not only Sigismondo's city but his lair. He designed and built the first castle intended to withstand artillery; and there he made his court which, though small, was one of the most cultured in Italy. Full of pride and invention in war, he set Valturio to write his famous *De re militari*.

Sigismondo won his way, soon to be the boldest as well as the most incalculable soldier of his time. No task, no trouble, no privation was too great for him when in the mood. But his means were never equal to the scale he required. The Tempio is the solid manifestation of an intense and lifelong vaunt. He was over-sized, he was the elephant caught in the small jungles of Italian policy.

Violent his life but not extravagant. His libertinage was sometimes terrible because undisguised. He did not favour insurance policies taken out with God or man. He did not justify his actions; since he thought he could transfuse anything into his blue day. Respected in Italy for his bravery and skill in war, his noble birth and his humanism, Sigismondo championed the interests of Pope Eugenius: the Florentine state owed him every-

The Tempio: First Visit

thing, the Venetians employed him time and time again. But he made good enemies. Spider-men knew at once their natural foe. Alfonso, king of Naples, frustrated in his attempt, one that had had prospect of success, to conquer Italy, frustrated by the irresponsibility, as he thought, and by the military genius of Sigismondo, became vindictive. Sigismondo got him on the quick, also Pope Pius II for whom the humbling of Sigismondo became an emotional need. In these vendettas causing his downfall, Sigismondo stimulated resentments out of proportion to their apparent causes. Not his behaviour alone, but his personality, amounted to a most penetrating reproach against anyone settling into a house: and, after the peace of Lodi, all Italy was settling in. Aragon had achieved Naples; Sforza Milan; Cosimo was firm in Florence; Venice had moderated her territorial ambition; Eugenius IV and Innocent V had made Rome habitable for popes.

Sigismondo's craftiness was too closely charged yet abrupt for his permanent success over more naïvely opportunist and, indeed, more cautious, contemporaries. Thus he desired for himself the sagacity of the elephant, choosing a large animal since he could not exercise moderation in a manner less astonishing than the one of elephants. In truth, each frustration added to his fury and to the scale of his designs. But he knew that patience and tact were virtues required for his triumph. Hence the wry and cumbersome motto 'Tempus tacendi, tempus loquendi'. At first, in the matter of Isotta, it was *tempus tacendi*, possibly because of the powerful and useful connections of his Sforza wife. A few years later it

Plate 41. Balustrade of Verona marble. Designed by Pasti.

Plate 42. Sigismondo Malatesta. Sculptor unknown.

was the full *tempus loquendi*, entailing the reinvestment of the whole of San Francesco, not ostensibly or primarily, it should be said, for the sake of Isotta, but according to the twin Greek inscriptions[1] on the encasement's flanks, to celebrate his triumphs in war. This phase was closed finally by Pio's denunciation,[2] excommunication and crusade of 1461.

No amount of historical research provides us with 'the truth about Isotta', the nature of her spell over Sigismondo. We know little more than that he finally married her and that she was regent in Rimini when Venice sent him to Greece against the Turks on his last

---

[1] The inscriptions read as follows: Sigismondo Pandolfo Malatesta, son of Pandolfo, having survived many and vital dangers in the Italian war, bringer of victory (νικηφόρος), for the campaigns by him concluded with courage and good fortune, to immortal God and to the City has dedicated this Temple, and in raising it has shouldered with brave heart the immense expense, leaving a noble and sacred monument.

[2] It is upon the evidence of the denunciation and of the Ciceronian journalese of Pio's commentaries (thus, 'mulieres, quorum filios e sacro fonte levavit, complures adulteriis polluit eorumque viros necavit'), in fact, upon the evidence of the purest war propaganda, that historians have acclaimed Sigismondo as a monster of crime. Yet for many years now Giovanni Soranzo has been examining these accusations and he has proved beyond doubt that the majority, at any rate, are baseless, in some cases, irreconcilable with the hard facts of time and place. Since he was somewhat out of scale with his contemporaries, calumny was the usual weapon of Sigismondo's foes: but Pio's denunciation and Federico di Montefeltro's tales carried little conviction in the Italy of that time until the political motive of the Malatesta crusade was revealed, that is to say, the seizure of his lands, and until a partition of the spoils had been promised. Cf. especially among the works of Soranzo *Un invettiva della curia romana contro Sigismondo Pandolfo Malatesta*, Imola, 1911. Also *Pio II e la politica italiana nella lotta contro I Malatesti*, 1457-1463. Drucker, Padua, 1911.

campaign; and that she was his heir. We gain no picture of Isotta from the Court eulogies: Renaissance poetry could tell nothing of the quality of Sigismondo's love. Yet we may know it even better than if we were living with both of them, since the dominant or underlying aspect of that love was projected, more or less unconsciously as I believe, in some of the Tempio masterpieces which it inspired. No direct approach elicits their full content. We shall feel the pressure of the emotion they exhibit only when we shall have found in what circumstance the fantasies of stone and water, of influence from the stars, and of the pervasive female seductiveness could be identified.

And so, we now leave the Tempio: but we must gather again in front of these representations of the planets to collect an entirely different concourse of words, which, joined to those already in our possession, will form a new and final likeness of these reliefs, the most magnetic part of Agostino's work.

Chapter Six

Chapel of the Planets

I had scarcely entered the church when my eye was caught by the reliefs of Diana, Mercury and Venus up the aisle (Pl. 24). They are not in a good light as seen from the door, yet owing to the manner in which they compose together and to the technique of their cutting that I have described, these figures swim, luminous, phosphorescent. But that is not all. Their *meaning* at once engages attention. Under the guise of planets we here see the first reappearance, after the dark centuries, of real pagan gods and goddesses, Diana, Mercury, Venus, Mars, Jupiter, Saturn. Agostino's Quattro Cento technique causes their reappearing as planets to possess the quality of a materialization, an exorcism. A spell works that keeps the forms swimming about in the marble like goldfish in a tank. And if their draperies more often seem disconcerted by water influence rather than by wind, the limbs beneath are greedy for air penetrating the blood, for the breeze of mysterious spring, which, though intangible, is closely allied to the breath of prophecy and to the dance. In the best of these reliefs the pagan spirit is re-created from its very source: what lay separate in Greek myth, in Greek life, in Greek sculpture, after long storage in the yearning heart appears concentrated with the full force of rediscovery; a pagan essence, undiluted, snatched from Time's filter. Thus the past can be concentrated, by virtue of a synthetic act which is more closely creation than re-creation. The process is everlasting. Out of the synthesis performed by Agostino, upon the synthesis which in his time passed as the conception of the Ancient World, I now create another.

From where comes the strength of his fantasy, from where the spell? Is it some inheritance of the vivid Etruscan religions in their treatment of Greek deities? Is it an Etruscan incantation, brought to the light, if not of the sun, then of the moon, by the vital and generous Renaissance spirit?

We must not forget the thousand years or more of Christianity that divided the Renaissance from pagan Rome.

How does Diana return? (Pls. 13, 44). From the woods of the soul yet pagan as ever. But where now is the dryness of the too habitual pagan nakedness? Gone. Diana comes greyish out of a black sky, out of a mist of apparel. A bucolic maiden she is upon the platform of her chariot, wheels and horses grinding a bank of cloud, in her hand the unaccustomed crescent of the moon which shows to the below as she drives across the firmament. Is she a Gothic wench, inflated by night airs into the round, or has the stateliness of the hollow classic Diana suffered the compression of youth? For certainly there is compression about her form and, in spite of the inspired tenuous attitude, every part of her body is running close

Plate 43. Angel holding up canopy on wall of first chapel to the right.

Plate 44. Diana.

to her middle. Her bucolic roundness is slender, she is, indeed, compressed with grace. For she has a soul, a delicacy that needs must be tense when issuing to meet the solid, to impregnate the cool and rough natural world. So Diana works with concentrated grace to hold the heavy, rinded, moon over her journey. No figure coming so deep from the marble would spring angular or slick. There has been tightness in the bound: her nose is broad like bulbs that have broken earth. She is an apparition. Eyes in those peasant features are full of space, expression of the half-aroused hypnotic. For she has been summoned out of the marble as if by trumpets, shrill trumpets that drown the murderous bugles of the Last Judgment, so that starlight now specks the darkness of her mind. Ripple of drapery over her skin as the folds unwrap to linger with the breeze arouses her from trance. What is this new nakedness? Eyes, all eyes. A leg, voluble as are eyes of youthfulness, of grace. An exteriorization of divinity, not an exterior, this arduous nudity. . . .

The conception 'soul' is entirely different from the $\psi\upsilon\chi\acute{\eta}$[1] of the Greeks to which it is made to correspond. For the word 'soul' indicates an entity conceived not merely to serve as a nucleus that survives the body, but as that for which the body is an expression rather than the unmatched encasement. Hence, too, our other conception, that of personality, unknown to the Ancients; hence *virtù*, an indispensable word to Cavalcanti and to

---

[1] Not, perhaps, as found in Plato and after Plato. I shall have something to say further on about the inadequacy of Plato as an interpreter of Greek spirit.

all Italians after him, a word that indicates the character of a human being, or even of an object, the essence that is manifested in every attribute. Further, the idea of destiny, Fate, as inherent not adherent, not stumbled upon as in Greek tragedies. Comparatively speaking, the Ancients were inattentive to eyes just as they were to 'soul'. Their emphasis upon the exterior (though it is really no such thing because they did not thus seek to hide an interior), the absence, then, of shadow, of modulation, which prolonged wooing of the classics can reveal, is finally distasteful to many people. They hate the rippling bodies that step and bend down the museum's long corridor. Their effect is flat, like palms that prophesy immovable in the breeze, or like the moon-grabbing gestures of cacti. And, in so far as Christianity enunciates a concomitance, a shadow, an emphatic intrusion of tenderness or guilt, a gesture of grace that hardly existed before, so far, and no further, Christianity has given a stamp to consciousness that will take some time to erase.

And long since at the temple of Athene in Syracuse, the columns have been squeezed inside walls to make a cathedral, and the cella has been cut into low rough arches to resemble a nave. Taller than these arches, tremendous on columns wedged between courses of the outer walls, on the inside caged and tamed by Christian sounds, Doric drums yet pound music as do the helpless projections in a sea-cavern that tapers to an obscure recess. Great the noise of the columns, incense from the low nave cannot shadow their whiteness. But confusing their beat, the organ peals the brown Gregorian chant;

and though the tide of the service cannot obliterate their
pagan countenance, yet that full tide makes of them a
thing dead, though loud in death, like barking pebbles
beneath the surf, monoliths beyond the clutch of soul,
masks of non-comprehension. For has not the ear inclined to the dance of dead leaves, to the note of birds?
Does not the sky droop from the vault of heaven, cowled
in tenderness?

Christianity externalized a spiritual omnipotence
which clouded the clear and concrete light of paganism.
Our conception of paganism, of course, is an abstraction which helps to isolate the values which most faith-
fully mirror the Mediterranean climate and geography.
It was the same Mediterranean clear light at its
strongest into which the medieval world was compelled
by the Quattro Cento spirit. Then there grew an even
greater love for stone as the symbol of objectivity. It was
needed. For that which was to be made concrete by the
light was vast and long-accumulated. The feelings that
overcast the pagan world are here called Christian; the
difference between classic Greek culture as a Mediterranean expression and the Quattro Cento as a Mediterranean expression are here ascribed to the Christianity
of the intervening centuries. This is certainly one point
among many, but as certainly it is not the most comprehensive. There is a deeper cultural trend connected
with older beliefs. They existed in the pagan world along
with our abstraction, the Mediterranean culture, over
which they soon triumphed. I refer to astrology and
other cosmological religions. Curiously enough in the
Quattro Cento, the purer paganism was reasserted

always at the instance of cosmological ideas with which it had been inextricably confused. Thus Diana and the other immortals appear in these reliefs as stars accompanied by the signs of the Zodiac.

Some scholars have held that all mythology, and particularly the Greek, contains astrological reference. How far this is true does not concern us. Whatever the origin of their myths, the Greeks developed them into Mediterranean poetry; and the cosmological aspects of their religions reflected the non-continental, the Mediterranean life. The Mediterranean quality bred an attitude rather than any specific dogma. If, unlike dogma, it is impossible to sweep away attitude as such, it is yet easily and subtly diverted from more creative, to less creative, beliefs. Through the medium of the Roman empire, oriental cosmological religions, even in classical times, began to oust what we have considered to be the purer Mediterranean paganism. The Roman empire, the Romans themselves, were not by any means a typical growth of Mediterranean climate. Unlike all the other great Mediterranean peoples, the Romans were not by nature seafaring. In Latium, as in Bœotia, the bulk of the people lived on fertile land in the interior. Rome took to sea to fight Carthage and the Tyrrhenian pirates. There is something almost continental about the scale of the Roman Campagna. There was something continental, Asiatic, about the Roman empire from its earliest days. Soon, very ancient oriental religions found favour at Rome, religions that had already permeated Alexander's Hellenistic world, preparing the way for Christianity around the Mediterranean itself. Again, I must remark that what I have attempted to isolate as being the Mediterranean values, have rarely found specific projection except in art, supremely so in Quattro Cento art. But even in this case, the Mediterranean content is expressed by that very power to make concrete rather than always in the ideas and theories thus objectified. More generally, and in varying degrees, Mediterranean values have served to provide such an aesthetic measure in outlook as afforded continental dogmas their most (aesthetically) complete expression. The Mediterranean always gives art to life, to any life. The Mediterranean attitude heightened to the pitch of a dogma for which art and life are judged by the same standards, we ascribe to the Greeks of the Persian wars alone and, in a slightly confused if more vehement way, to the men of the Quattro Cento. And since the Greeks came first, they have become the ever-attractive symbol of sunlight, health, reasonableness and culture. That very reasonableness, of course, inherent in the attitude, causes it but rarely to attain the overbearing strength of dogma; with the result that in weaker moments it has been a prey to foreign dogmas.

After the Alexandrine conquests, Semitic dogma invades the Mediterranean world, particularly in the form of astrological beliefs. These same beliefs, which had been connected up with the more purely pagan gods and goddesses of Greece and Rome, survived within Christianity. Under such distorted forms paganism has a part in medieval culture, and in this disguise the gods appear openly, and not as Christian devils, at the time of the Renaissance. Thus, in an attempt to reach true paganism, the Renaissance men studied astrology with which paganism was confused.

These cultural threads are brought together and objectified by the planet reliefs. They contain the startling reappearance of Greek-myth figures, the vehement concentration of what is purely Mediterranean, and at the same time, an assembly of something vastly old and more comprehensive (it swallowed the Greek), a meaning unwrapped from several thousand years of culture and here put outward as the Quattro Cento spirit alone could manage. The concretion itself, born of clear light, is a Mediterranean content; even if that light is not the sun but the moon. Yet the meaning thus shown is not so entirely Mediterranean; though it is the highest proof of the Mediterranean compulsion to make manifest, to make the stone alive, when easily and naturally it incorporated in Quattro Cento carving so ancient and so metaphysical a reference. On the other hand, I am convinced that the Quattro Cento carving as a whole is partly dependent on this metaphysical meaning. Hence the supreme importance of the planet reliefs in which alone[1] this meaning has direct visual expression. We shall find that it is a meaning which, by the time of the 15th century, had been finally reduced to Mediterranean terms, and thereupon not only assisted the intensifica-

[1] There are other and later marble representations of the signs of the Zodiac, as, for instance, those carved on the base of the pillars in the Piazza Vittorio Emmanuele at Ravenna. But these lack all esoteric significance. The lovely frescoes of the signs of the Zodiac in the Trinci palace at Foligno date from a few years earlier than the Tempio reliefs. The Trinci conception, however, is medieval rather than Renaissance.

tion of the Mediterranean feeling for stone and for its connection with water, but to so great an extent encouraged this feeling and was identified with it that without such aid, carving would not have become so vital, nor Agostino's surfaces have been so intricate, nor his flattening of form so pronounced.

Of what kind the metaphysical, or, rather, cosmological, meaning that is so mixed up with the reappearance of Diana and the others from the stone at Rimini, that they needs must reappear as planets, amid the attendant signs of the Zodiac?

I am led back to the Babylonian night. Each night from the earliest history I would now recall. Far more than in the days, in the nights the most different cultures have shared common fantasies and edifices of thought to contain the universe. By the stars and by the luminaries, not alone the days, the weeks, the months, the seasons were reckoned and named, but terrestrial things also—all terrestrial life was subject to these regular convolutions of light-points in the sky, to their conjunctions, to their oppositions, their decline, their rise, their angles of longitude, sextile, sesquiquadrate, biquintile.

To our civilization which has gradually modified the egocentric position—it dies hard for it is the condition of all simple poetry—to us whose astronomy reveals distances and sizes which reject the human measure and which thus oppose 'straightforward' imaginative construction, to us it may seem strange that men so long attributed such close terrestrial influence to the faint stars and to the small bright stars. What fantasy is this that they regulate our lives? To deify the sun is comprehensible. The sun is the supreme power on the earth. To deify the moon is understandable. But these small stars with which some nights are sprinkled, how were they imagined, and universally imagined, to ordain the courses of life?

There is a weather at sea when the wind shrieks and waters topple but the sky is clear and hard. On such a night, while the sail smacks like a hooked shark, there is above it a studded unruffled sky bathed for an expanse in the vapourous wash of the milky way. The stars are firm in the blackness of the night; and guiding your tossing ship by their silent journeys, you may draw near in thought to Plato's image of the cave. In point of order, the earthly happening seems the shadow of those clear courses to which each generation has looked for the determination of time and place.

Soon, the structure of knowledge and of culture already gained from observance of the stars was extended by the attribution of powers. After all, the seasons answered to the appearance and disappearance of the constellations; the growth and wane of the moon influenced the shapes and sizes of oysters.[1] Men too were subject to the almost liquid influence of stellar determination.

The heavenly bodies are the only objects known to us outside the earth. It was unlikely that transcendental speculation should omit to consider those bodies whose movements answered to the divine and mysterious science of mathematics. Pascal, we know, was frightened of stellar space, and so should we be if we stood, as he

[1] Cf. Augustine, *Civ. Dei*, 5, 6.

Chapel of the Planets

did, near the brink of the Industrial Age. XVIIth-century Pascal was far nearer to the myth and to the evidence of the senses, clung closer than we can to the simple human projection. At the same time, Pascal's science was near enough to our own to be badly equipped with imaginative satisfactions. But in ancient times speculation was infinitely less separated from some naïve wish-fulfilment; and if we would understand any 'system', whether of science or philosophy, before the 16th century at the earliest, we must ourselves experience the pleasure of exciting universal deductions mixed in with factual observation. Heretofore the wise man has been the knowledgeable man. Everything answered to a system. The most abstract speculation could appear vital. Naturally, astrology and astronomy were one. Sidereal considerations exercised the minds of the most thoughtful men for several thousand years. And who shall say they were wrong in the importance they attached to the stars? The modern astronomer tells us that radiation is the guiding principle of the universe and of all universes; that probably matter itself is a form of radiation; that the earth is pelted, we are pelted, continually by stellar radiation whose effect no one has yet measured. Still more in keeping with old doctrines is the recent tendency of physics to describe the universe in terms of waves. Matter is composed of waves that move in circles, radiation in straight lines. If we add images of Einsteinian curvature of space and of the compression in shape which speed effects on bodies, we obtain a picture that reminds us of the parabolas and fusing segments in any astrological chart, the heavy lore of which is embodied freely in stone at Rimini. For compression and flattening of shape, as we have seen, was characteristic of Agostino's technique, especially in the reliefs of the planets; and there is not a marble by his hand that has subsided. Every form is potent, compressed, distorted, circles into ovoids, squares into cylinders: ferment and interaction are directly expressed by the interlacing of straight and bending planes.

The twelve signs of the Zodiac, that is to say, the names of twelve constellations whose habitats were associated with regions of the sky that vaguely corresponded for each month of the year with the sun's ecliptic, were invented about 2800 B.C. This we know because precession has carried round the 'first point of Aries' as we now call it, the point where the sun is at the spring equinox, some sixty-six degrees, corresponding to 4730 years. The latitude in which the Zodiac was first mapped out can be reckoned from the range of these twelve and thirty-six other associated constellations, which were all that were known—that is to say, all that were within the horizon. Roughly speaking the latitude is N.38°. The longitude cannot be deduced. But many paths of research lead one back to Babylon. We know from their cuneiform that the Chaldeans were advanced in astronomical computation on which their religious beliefs were based, we know the Ancient World looked to Mesopotamia for astronomy and for prediction. Egypt took its heavens from Babylon, and Magian thought, whether identified or dissociated or bastardized amid current religions, was the principal common ground of Europe and Asia from the earliest times until the middle of the 16th century A.D. The idea of 'the Oriental' is a modern idea. Hitherto, both in Europe and in Asia, science and magic, calculation and prophecy, were always near to one another. Mathematics could at any moment be pregnant with a non-mathematic meaning, just as each bare geometric movement of the stars was thought to sustain some corpus of particular embodiment on earth below.

One wonders how much this last fantasy has to do with the apparitions at Rimini and with representational art as a whole. As far as Semitic representation is concerned, it probably has a lot to do. An embodiment of Grecian vales, each grove, each brook, could always be an anthropomorphic projection, realized in sculpture by human forms. But what gods to satisfy a civilized people could be construed out of the fierce Mesopotamian expanse, how should the deserts be conducted to corporeal stature?

The Chaldean did not know he was bumping through space. At night, when he stood on a white tower above the plain, it seems he clawed in his mind the immediate canopy above. The moon rode there, a clear orb. The moon was a masculine principle and took precedence of the sun. The moon's bald steadiness in enlargement and diminution, such nightly convolution of shape, so many visible yet preternatural courses, aroused every instinct that showed as a desire to make measurements. The supreme drama was the constant animus of the planets as they moved in opposition to all other celestial bodies and passed unwinking from the night. No wonder that to those five wanderers or

Chapel of the Planets

planets, Mercury, Venus, Mars, Jupiter, Saturn, together with the moon and sun, all human destiny was entrusted. No wonder their aspects in reference to the constellations through which they pass have always been the whole subject-matter of astrology.

Yet one may still be amazed that the stars were thought no less powerful in the day. How, at all, could they be associated with the day and with the sun's ecliptic? Venus, it is true, may sometimes be observed even at high noon: a transit of Venus must have caused the Chaldean who slept in the sun to be aroused acutely. There has always been a tradition that, given suitable circumstances, stars are visible in the day. Aristotle mentions that observers had seen stars in daylight when looking out from caverns or subterranean reservoirs. Pliny advises deep wells for daytime astronomy.

But it was foremost the dramatic eclipse that proved the stars to be constant in sunlight. When the sun was veiled, the deeper reality of the pulsating cosmic forces was apparent. A total eclipse of the sun was a moment of supreme suspense. It was as if the skies themselves suffered the expectant shudder, exerted the frigid, constant, will with which the heavy world wrests each dawn. A modern astronomer[1] must write as follows of a total eclipse: "As the eclipse advances, but before the totality is complete, the sky grows of a dusky livid, or purple, or yellowish-crimson colour, which gradually gets darker and darker, and the colour appears to

[1] Sir Norman Lockyer, K.C.B., *Elementary Lessons in Astronomy*, Macmillan, 1919.

214

run over large portions of the sky, irrespective of the clouds. The sea turns livid red. This singular colouring and darkening of the landscape is quite unlike the approach of night, and gives rise to strange feelings of sadness. The moon's shadow is seen to sweep across the surface of the earth, and is even seen in the air; the rapidity of its motion and its intenseness produce a feeling that something material is sweeping over the earth at a speed perfectly frightful. All sense of distance is lost, the faces of men assume a livid hue, fowls hasten to roost, flowers close, cocks crow, and the whole animal world seems frightened out of its usual propriety."

The principles of the sky were uniformity and recurrence. Unusual phenomena were the more unusual, and so, preternaturally ominous. As a prologue and an epilogue to each sidereal display, meteorological effects were no doubt watched. There was the dawn and the sunset and the rainbow, each harping upon many meanings. Then there happened the phenomena that can follow a gigantic volcanic eruption, afterglows, foreglows, sun-pillars, luminous night-clouds, Bishop's ring. Following the eruption of Krakatoa in 1883, the sun was seen to be blue or green in Batavia, in Ceylon, at various places in India; "blue when at the zenith, changing through green and yellow to total obscuration near the horizon".[1] It is unlikely, though, that similar phenomena seen in Babylon would have been regarded as meteorological. On the other hand, clouds that but mask with cirrus or with their furious volumes the brilliancy of the pointed

[1] *Astronomy without a Telescope*, E. W. Maunder, F.R.A.S., London, 1902.

stars, found no place in astrological reckoning. Conversely, of course, in northern atmospheres where the clouds were so often banked, the celestial theatre was not at first envisaged: whereas the northern diviners watched the passage of the clouds themselves for omens.

The stars had little or no place in Doric religion: a further reason for thinking the Dorians to have come from the North. In Egypt, too, astrology was unknown before the 6th century B.C., though among the Egyptians, as among more primitive peoples, the sun and moon were official deities. As far back as the 15th century B.C., Amenophis IV ordained an exclusive worship of the sun. In Greece no official identification was made between deities and celestial points before the 4th century B.C. The Homeric names for the five planets reflect the qualities of their respective lights only.

Aristophanes, says Franz Cumont,[1] characterized the difference between the religion of the Greeks and that of the barbarians by observing that the latter sacrifice to the sun and moon, the former to personal divinities like Hermes. On the other hand, the existing pre-Hellenic population no doubt shared the worship of the 'barbarians'. And also the philosophers found the essence of things among the stars. But not even the Platonic conception of the firmament was used in contemporary religion. The cities built their temples for personable gods and goddesses. No doubt many of them were sidereal by origin, had been translated downward to serve localities on earth. In many cities, the ruling Greek class of the 5th century, as reflected by their reli-

[1] *Astrology and Religion among the Greeks and Romans*, Putnam, 1912.

gion, appears to have been in a middle position between the philosophers or mystics and the common people or slaves, in touch with both but belonging to neither. So bourgeois a position may easily coincide, in small communities at any rate, with that of the poet and artist, and, indeed, come to be largely governed by aesthetic standards. The solid yet beautiful anthropomorphism of Hellas, one feels, was the happiest expression of bourgeois domination. The cities forwent cosmopolitan or barbarian and princely *cachet*. They wanted rural and suburban gods, and gods of the seas for their merchandise. So habitable are the stone-lit lands that not even death sends the spirit upward. In Greece, when the summer sun goes spinning at full noon, goat and olive odour draws you to the ground and the deep-welling spring. The spell of shade, of wine, of sleep, wherever you have clambered, draws you to the bosom of the earth, to vales and fields within the earth. There the Elysian flats, there the Tartarean night.

The soul will move differently in huge Mediterranean towns that have impaired the sense of neighbourhood. In his *Dream of Scipio*, Cicero imagines deserving souls rising to the stars. For he had watched the stars over the cold roofs of a vast Rome, had felt the beat of his own heart; and there above him were projected as nuclear brightnesses consuming the hard, incorporeal night, the souls of heroes which on earth had been overt yet invisible sparks.

Cicero, of course, should not thus be characterized as a town-dweller. But it is true to say that by his time Mediterranean culture had become far less local in spirit, far more cosmopolitan. There is reason to believe that Plato, who taught that the stars were divine animations of the Demiurge, received a 'Chaldean' guest who instructed him in his old age.[1] And, indeed, the Timaeus doctrine of the soul that passes through the planetary system before physical birth, probably reflects some earlier Babylonian contact, direct or otherwise. Henceforward, oriental science penetrates the West, even though specific astrological prediction is rejected. Alexander's conquests created the cosmopolitan situation politically. The points of the nocturnal skies alone were common, or nearly common, throughout that empire which men traversed with guidance from those stars. Star-worship alone could be the religious bond of such an empire; and in relation to a star, local myths of the same intent were mingled so as to accept a distant colour and redoubled dramatization. In Greece the planets became the stars of Hermes, Aphrodite, Ares, Zeus, Kronos,[2] because these gods roughly corresponded to the Babylonian planet-deities, Nebo, Ishtar, Nergal, Marduk and Ninib. Later, the Phrygian cult of Cybele and Attis was equated to the myth of Venus and Adonis: later still, Attis became a solar god just as did other foreign deities like Serapis, the Baals and Mithra.

Such transformations are of importance to the history of medieval and Renaissance astrological thought: for the character attributed to each planet and to the signs

[1] Cf. Cumont, *op. cit.*, p. 49, and his comments on a note to this effect preserved in a papyrus of Herculaneum.

[2] The Latin names derived from these are the ones we use.

of the Zodiac, and the symbols attached to them, reflected a vast content of the most diverse myth-equation.

In Hellenistic Greece "'Catasterism', that is, translation to the stars, became a convenient method of giving an astronomical termination to ancient fables. Thus poetical tales, which were only half believed, represented fabulous heroes and even members of human society as living on high in the form of glittering constellation. There Perseus found Andromeda again, and the centaur Chiron, who is none other than the Archer, fraternized with Orion. The Ram was the famous ram with the Golden Fleece who had carried off Phrixus and Helle over the sea and had let the maiden fall into the waves of the Hellespont. It might also be that which was a subject of the dispute between Atreus and Thyestes, or again it might be the ram which guided the thirsty company of Bacchus to the wells of the oasis of Ammon."[1]

Stoicism was a semi-oriental cult. The Stoics believed fire to be the first principle and regarded the stars as its supreme manifestation. The next famous name in Stoicism after Zeno of Tarsus, the founder, is Diogenes of Babylon. "Zeno", says Cicero,[2] "attributed a divine power (*vis divina*) to the stars, but also to the years, the months and the seasons." Here we have a simple example of measurement and, indeed, of the principle of order, intertwined with projected fantasy and dogma. No conglomeration of modern fantasies can attain such dignified rational projection. To a far greater extent our fantasies are destined to remain fantasies

[1] Cumont, *op. cit.*   [2] Cic. *De Nat. Deor.*, II, 63.

without acceptable, that is to say, without seemingly objective or rationalized, projection. Analogy to human response has less and less relevance in the world of modern science, and in the environment it creates. We employ so many forces that seem in no sense a projection of ourselves. This environment causes the emotional change which profoundly separates us, not from this or that, but from all the centuries together: or so it seems if we overlook the fact that this change has developed slowly all the time from the Renaissance: as early as 1770, it is already near to being apprehended. England was the first country to enter the Industrial Age. At the same time the Romantic poets arose. It was in England that the first conscious protest was made to preserve what was already the old sense of ritual; that the first nostalgia for an emblematic (human-analogy) environment appeared. We laugh at the neo-Gothic: all its later stages were so false. We laugh at pre-Raphaelitism and whatever corresponds to it to-day. Still, the question remains: how to interpret modern environment and condition as the rationalized projection of ourselves. For all poetry, all art, all culture, are projections of ego-centric attitude. Civilization is harnessed passion, and culture has been the recompense and the mode for sublimated desire. Whereas civilization has needed to develop the conception of scientific necessity, culture has extracted poetry from the very fact itself of 'pure' thought. Science, we now find, can be too pure for culture. Perhaps we belong to the past, just because all *our* possible values are weakening: perhaps art and other reputable projections of fantasy will no longer satisfy:

perhaps it will be all to the good (for the future generations): perhaps the machine is the instrument of the change (unconsciously planned and desired by us as well), rather than the Frankenstein it otherwise would appear to be.

Whatever the answer, it is certain that measurement or science was originally the instrument of religious or philosophic revelation. Calendars had a religious, before acquiring a secular, meaning. For measurement in those days, of whatever force or magnitude or dimension, always took as the reference point of force, magnitude or dimension, the human organism. Whatever such science revealed was a commentary upon man and upon his efforts. Science was almost poetry. . . .

Augustus as well as Tiberius was a convert to astrology. Posidonius of Apamea, some hundred and fifty years before their time, had mixed Grecian and Asiatic thought to such good purpose as to erect a vast appliance of sidereal cosmogony, a constellation of sectarian doctrines that seemed to shine universally. His pantheistic thought was welcomed by the upper classes in Rome and gradually infected the populace among whom passed the clergy and the devotees of oriental cults. "Astrological paganism deified the active principles which move all celestial and terrestrial bodies. Water, fire, earth, the sea, and the blast of winds, but above all the luminous heavens of the fixed stars and planets revealed the boundless power of the God who filled all nature. But this pantheism no longer naïvely regarded this nature as peopled by capricious spirits and unregulated powers. Having become scientific, it conceived the gods as cosmic energies, the providential action of which is ordered in a harmonious system."[1] We see how well the ground was prepared for the triumph of Christianity.[2] Especially important in this connection is the neo-Platonic doctrine of a supreme divinity infusing Nature, yet itself existent also outside Nature. Philo the Jew reproached the Chaldeans with worshipping the creation instead of the creator. He could hardly have reproached Plato on this account. For Plato was the least Greek of all the Greeks. The Chaldeans, Semitic though they were, managed to be better polytheists, better humanists and pagans than did he.

Mithraic sun-worship was the final political form that Roman paganism assumed. Heliogabalus proclaimed himself the sun on earth and emperor in his fifteenth year. He is called *Sol Invictus Elagabal* in inscriptions. He was soon assassinated; but fifty years later Aurelian renewed the doctrine of the emperor as the sun, with complete success. *Sol Invictus* walks the earth until the death of his ultimate incarnation, Julian the Apostate.

The side of antique thought I have discussed affords the approach not only into the medieval mind, but also to the world of the Humanists. After making some reference to medieval astrology I shall have then created the background as I see it of 15th-century culture. The revival of Learning was the revival of Pantheism, neo-Platonic, neo-Babylonian, neo-Aristotelian.

[1] Cumont, *op. cit.*, p. 123.

[2] On the other hand, the determinism implicit in all astrological doctrine and in all prediction passed intact to Mohammedanism.

Chapel of the Planets

This statement is not based solely upon the dull works of the Humanists themselves. I find it impossible to interpret fully the sculpture in the Tempio or, indeed, any Quattro Cento sculpture without inducing this cultural background. The unconscious Mediterranean feeling for stone and for its connections with water needed for their paramount realization some specific doctrine to which it could attach itself. I do not intend anything so foolish as that 15th-century sculptors were students of astrology, though astrological belief was increasingly popular in that time. I refer solely to the specific images that were then current in men's minds. The relation between astrological image and fantasies inspired by stone, is equally well seen from either side. I do not now argue about precedence. I wish to point only to the coincidence, the identification and the mutual reinforcement at work in the matter of these two groups of fantasies to which I attribute the unexampled vitality of Quattro Cento sculpture. Think how the stone was carved to disclose forms that appear as if responding to some influence. In many Quattro Cento reliefs the movement of figures suggests a response to magnetic power. To wind and water are attributed the most flamboyant impulsions. Shells come up from the sea to line a door jamb: and there they stick encrusted. All Nature is alive, all concrete things show sidereal powers of influence. *Sol Invictus* has a thousand incarnations. Flowers strain their fighting roots to lie open: dolphins plunge in air. These fantasies are solid stone.

They may seem far removed from anything the dour sidereal motions might suggest, beyond the general idea of 'influence'. But there is one connecting link which is all-important. This is the philosophy of Aristotle which, so far as it was known, dominated later medieval thought. Aristotle considered the stars to be made of a quintessential element, and the sublunary world to be made of combinations and permutations of the four elements, fire, air, earth and water. The medieval and Renaissance image for permutations was of something liquid. The essences distilled in retorts by medieval doctors, the *aqua vitae* for which they searched, the transmutation of metals that was demanded from the boiling cauldron, reflect this image of change through transfusion. The very influence of the stars upon the fates of men was imagined as a suctional force to which bodies must respond: and so far as concrete things were thought vital, they too would incorporate in their mass tumultuous waves that were the images of life and movement. From this side of medieval image, we again see the connection between stone and water. In Quattro Cento sculpture the four elements exert their powers upon one another and change their attributes; or man expresses his new abundant vigour by giving them in charge to uproarious putti who ransack the surfaces of the stone.

We are familiar with the quick fecundity of the stone and its association with moisture. These fierce permutations of force and freshness, as well as the tense riot of putti, suggest to me some deep assurance in a compulsive dynamic cycle, some rock-like thesis of change. The most distinct and prosaic form of this poetry is undoubtedly the medieval divagation upon Aristotle's physics of motion.[1] Aristotelian transformations of physical bodies had their origin in the stars. The stars were the prime movers, the source of growth and change and dissolution. The fixed stars were the rulers of permanence and growth, while the wide-circling planets were the dispensers of change and fitfulness. Both principles are found projected at a tension in Quattro Cento stone. In Quattro Cento architecture and sculpture I see the vivid stone as an immediate and universal solidity into the spatial terms of which is transmuted a fierce compulsive motion.

I have concentrated on the cosmological aspect of astrology, the source of its strength. Astrology to-day is more often conceived solely as a method of prediction from the stars. This practice, an outcome of the cosmological doctrine, has been in every age the butt of an easy ridicule, at any rate when precise and particular prediction was claimed. As for horoscope, Augustine and other Church fathers pointed to the differing fortunes of twins, or repeated the arguments of Carneades (219-126 B.C.) which were handed down as the leaven for all subsequent ridicule whether of Augustine, of Petrarch, of Pico della Mirandola or of Swift in his famous joke against the astrologer Partridge. But how-

[1] I may point out here that there is a connection too with Quattro Cento painting. In my final volume I shall make out a case for asserting that Giorgione directly expressed neo-Aristotelian doctrines in one or two of his extant paintings which there is reason to think were commissioned by young members of the Venetian aristocracy, a group led by Almorò Barbaro who was engaged on translating Aristotle for the first time from the original Greek.

ever much, in the Dark Ages and in medieval times, the Church fathers and others might condemn astrology of every kind, yet there remained in their writings admissions—so deep was the root of this belief—that the stars possessed some physical influence on the earth. Who could deny it altogether when the sun poured down and the Ptolemaic system worked? Cicero in the *De Divinatione* opposed genethlialogical or judicial prediction. On the other hand he wrote the *Somnium Scipionis*. Augustine, the arch-opponent of astrology because it represented the nucleus of paganism in the world that Christianity conquered, and because of the determinism[1] implicit in stellar influence, admits in one passage at least[2] the power of the stars over physical bodies, and even betrays a belief in the possibility of astrological prediction by attributing such power to demons. Augustine's attitude was adopted by the Church for many centuries. Thus we see that Christianity did not uproot paganism, but just sat on top of it. Pagan rite became magic—with the re-introduction of science by the Jews and Moors —often black magic. We can now easily envisage the atmosphere of medieval science, the fever of a magic perpetual motion, of the hot and hoary transformation of metals into gold, the treatise written near the potent

[1] Augustine's attitude is a little unequal on this point, since he combats astrological determinism only to put the determinism of predestination in its place. Those who, like Cicero, deny prediction altogether are more violently condemned by Augustine than are even the astrologers. Augustine's attitude shows how deeply entrenched, at the evolution of the medieval world, was the last astrological phase of paganism.

[2] See page 210.

crucible at the risk of the Church's stake, of her open
piazza fires.

But the Church gradually accepted Aristotle: it was
not alone fear of the Church that made science so dark,
so fibrous, tough and hoary. It was Christianity itself
that prevented the greater number of men from calm
or respectful worship of the creation. Christianity was
fevered, yet cold to the eye like the crucible in which
metal seethed. Men cackled at their bodies. Something
fearful is better overcome in the Renaissance. Paganism of a sort wells up unimpaired: the stars return to a
triumphant march: even the older paganism appears
once more for a flash. Artemis, Hermes and Aphrodite
have come down to Rimini after long transfiguration in
the skies.

From another angle, we may envisage medieval
thought as a steady march toward Renaissance. The
first awakening was in the 11th century at the school of
Chartres. It was here that science was reborn. Astrology
at once arose from that darkness to which Isidore of
Seville, the most uncompromising[1] of its opponents, had
committed it in the 7th century. Previous to the 11th
century, what was known of astrology was equated with
magic, since the only source of this knowledge was the
denunciations and admissions of the Church fathers. At
Chartres, William of Conches and others studied the
Mathesis of Firmicus Maternus and the neo-Platonic
commentaries of Chalcidius and Macrobius. As early as

[1] Yet Isidore admitted the relevance to medicine of stellar
observation. See *The Medieval Attitude toward Astrology, particularly in
England*, T. O. Wedel, Oxford Univ. Press, 1920.

1000 Pope Sylvester II had read Firmicus in Spain. Bernard Silvestris in his *De Mundi Universitate*, which he wrote between 1145 and 1153, sought to clear astrology of the magical essence with which the Church fathers confounded it. His conception was largely Platonic: he wrote of the ecstasy beneath the stars. But the introduction of the Arabic commentators, in the study of whose works Adelard of Bath was the pioneer in the 12th century, gave the trend we find typical of medieval thought. Plato of Tivoli had translated Ptolemy's *Tetrabiblos* into Latin in 1138. Purely Grecian astrology, however, was soon contaminated by the Arabic sources from which it now more usually came, and in which the demonology of the Talmud and the mysticism of the Cabala had been fused with the Grecian element. Not until the 15th century, and then only in visual art, in Quattro Cento art, is there attained a real and triumphant re-mingling and separation of Greek from Jew in his variously Hebraic, Christian and Arabic guises.

By 1200 large tracts of Aristotle had spread through Europe, translated from the Arabic. The Church was forced to compromise. But so long as determinism was rejected, there remained nothing truly foreign to ecclesiastical dogma in Aristotelian cosmology. And so, stellar influence on corporeal substance was less glossed over and more admitted. The interests of determinism and free will were adjusted in the various ways they can be adjusted, chiefly by Thomas Aquinas. Since Reason is not corporeal, argued Aquinas, it is not subject to the stars. Judicial astrology was still accounted the blackest magic, though some systems of prediction appeared less objectionable to the Church than others. Even in these matters the Church was very moderate; and the burning of the devout Cecco D'Ascoli, astrological professor at Bologna University in 1327, is unexpected and unexplained.

Roger Bacon, often accounted the father of modern science, believed in the existence of necromancy, that is to say, he condemned it. He thought that no specific predictions could otherwise be made from stars, but prediction not specific, that was concerned only with tendencies, might be made without necromancy.

The fortunes of judicial astrology are of little concern to the present argument. The point is that, though differing considerably in detail, all the medieval interpreters of Aristotle from Avicenna and Averroes to Albert the Great, Bartolomaeus Anglicus, Thomas Aquinas and Dante, accepted Aristotle's theory of motion.[1]

Before paganism went underground the Church had adopted the days of the week from astrology. The heavens were still there and the earth, after twelve centuries or so. It was as if the pagan stage had never been unsettled. The pagan characters of the 15th century assume their parts without ado.

The most positive characteristic of medieval thought to which Renaissance art was heir lay in the precision of images attached to philosophical terms. One feels more clearly in the case of Scholasticism than of other philosophies that the very scope of the problems that Schoolmen set themselves was defined by the domina-

[1] See page 225.

tion of certain images. However abstract their argument, a concept, whether of substance or of relation, was associated, and sometimes identified, with a visual form.[1] This well-matched alliance between dominant imagery and concepts made possible the supreme poetic achievement of Dante. Nor were the Elizabethans too late to express an abstract term succinctly with the language of visual impression.

Literature of no kind, however, can attain the tensity, the immediacy of presentation that is the distinctive virtue of visual art. The planet reliefs are the outstanding expression of those visual images in the medieval mind that accompanied the conception of Aristotle's physics of motion. Probably my reference should now be made to a wider concept, the medieval conception of Relation *whose appropriate images were always connected with water.* Indeed, we begin to see that some remembrance of astrological paganism was the unacknowledged basis of all medieval thought. Fluidity, influence, confluence, effluence, are words that belong to medieval parlance in

[1] See Ezra Pound's *Guido Cavalcanti Rime*, Marsano, Genova, 1931. Writing on Medievalism he says: "We appear to have lost the radiant world where one thought cuts through another with clean edge, a world of moving energies . . . magnetisms that take form, that are seen, or that border the visible . . . For the modern scientist energy has no borders, it is a shapeless 'mass' of force; even his capacity to differentiate it to a degree never dreamed by the ancients has not led him to think of its shape or even its *loci*. The rose that his magnet makes in the iron filings does not lead him to think of the force in botanic terms, or wish to visualize that force as floral and extant (*ex stare*)." Because they inherited the medieval scheme of attributing a definite *virtù* to each substance, Quattro Cento sculptors were able without any expostulation to express stone nature by their carving, and to associate it with the definite form that had been attributed to an energy such as magnetism.

matters of Relation. In accordance with astrological thought, relations of all kinds were conceived as influences flowing between two or more objects. No wonder that a *Philosophy* of Love is the typical medieval extravagance, the basis of spirituality as well as the scaffold of erotic poetry! But no medieval sonnet, no canzone, could express devious Influence, whether of Love or of the Planets, with the instant poignancy of Agostino's carving. In the Tempio we *see* Influence: we do not gather it from an accumulation of words. At Rimini its liquid gradualness is laid out in stone. In the Renaissance, the reinforced visual impressions that had inspired medieval thought attain a complete, unqualified expression as visual art: the field of literature is left fallow, or left to grow but the more superficial crops.

I have shown above the analogy or concurrence between images that Aristotle's physics of motion, as a habit of mind, could inspire in a sculptor, and the common Mediterranean fantasies concerning the communion of stone and water, which he would also inherit. In Chapter IV I described the magnetism of Agostino's reliefs in terms of the connection between limestone and water, a connection built up throughout Chapters I, II and III. I have written of the undulations, the vortices, the suctional forces and the swimming forms in these reliefs. If now I can show that an image of liquid magnetism was not only the deep inspiration behind the sculptor's approach to the marble, was not only suitably identified with the astrological subject of the planet reliefs, but further, that the expression of this same liquid magnetism, consciously or unconsciously, was demanded by the very personality and personal situation of the sculptor's employer, then I have explained to my satisfaction how arose this occasion in which the deepest and oldest Mediterranean fantasies connected with limestone obtained their paramount expression: I have explained the strong sense one has of an influence at work throughout this series.

But before we can reach our conclusion we must carry the outline of astrology a little further, so that we may see what kind of hold the idea of Influence possessed on the first few generations of the 15th century, and with what new ideas and with what new practices it was associated.

For in the 15th century, astrology, both as an old cosmological science with pagan connections and as an existent setting before which more pagan, more joyous, gods might take the air again, was serving new trends of thought. At the same time, the practical consultation of astrologers was by no means on the wane. The interest in astrology at Bologna, for instance, was not confined to the university nor to philosophical aspects. But perhaps it was more typical of the 14th rather than the 15th century, when in 1303 the commune granted to a person who called himself Giovanni di Luna an annual pension, since he had served local agriculture so well by his predictions. In the 15th century it was a few princes in particular who put the greatest reliance upon astrological prediction, such as Bartolommeo Orsini, count of Pitigliano. Filelfo padded his adulatory poem, the *Sforziade*, with so many references to the stars, that even a professional astrologer[1] took it amiss. It is extremely doubtful, however, whether the hero of the poem, Francesco Sforza, that great realist, put any reliance on the stars, as did the Visconti, his predecessors in Milan. Court poets were at liberty, none the less, to describe his fate as thus determined, since by such poetic argument was the status of apotheosis best implied. This kind of elementary astrology was the ornament and the poetry, rather than a dogma, of 15th-century intellectual life. At the same time, there is no doubt that Sforza's successors at Milan, Galeazzo Maria and Ludovico il Moro, were passionate devotees of the stars. Typical, however, of a 15th-century devotee was Galeazzo's astute custom of declaring to his people predictions (perhaps regularly fabricated) that were unfavourable to his enemies. A document exists that shows Il Moro advising Innocent VIII, the Pope himself, to consult the celebrated astrologer Ambrogio Varese about the outcome of an illness.[2] At Mantua, Bartolommeo Manfredi was court astrologer, serving more than one generation of the Gonzaga family. There is a letter[3] (with a postscript of thanks for a brace of quails) from Manfredi to Ludovico Gonzaga, telling him at what hour it would be best to take his powder.

[1] Cf. Galeotto Marzio's *Invectiva in Franciscum Philelphum*, Vat. Cod. 3411, M.L. 147.

[2] See *Nuove ricerche e documenti sull'astrologia alla corte degli Estensi e degli Sforza*. F. Gabotto, Turin, 1891.

[3] *Bartolommeo Manfredi e l'astrologia alla corte di Mantova*. F. Gabotto, Turin, 1891. Manfredi was a pupil of the famous pedagogue Vittorino da Feltre, originator of the public school spirit. Manfredi designed the clock tower at Mantua.

Chapel of the Planets

Such extreme superstition, however, was not usual among Italian Renaissance princes. Astrology became a fashion in intellectual and court circles, largely because of its dimly pagan and definitely anti-Christian cultural background. More typical of 15th-century thought are the deductions that Galeotto Marzio drew from the stars. He was prosecuted in 1477 at Venice for ascribing the religious fitfulness of mankind to stellar movements. When Jupiter was in conjunction with Mercury, Christianity arose; with the Sun, Egyptian practices; with Mars, Chaldean; and with the Moon, it is the religion of anti-Christ. Now, according to Pope Pius II, Sigismondo was avowedly anti-Christian or, at any rate, anti-God. In view of the exaltation of the moon in the planet reliefs (an additional zodiacal sign is invented for the moon, and she is in far more evidence than the sun represented on the keystone of the arch), and of the lunar images which, as we shall see, prevail throughout the series, one wonders whether there is any connection between the doctrines of Marzio and the sculpture at Rimini. Did Sigismondo harbour some esoteric doctrine of the anti-Christ? There have been investigators who thought they found in the *Isotteis* of Basinio, composed at Sigismondo's court in honour of his mistress, more than one hint of esoteric rite and symbolic manipulation staged in the Tempio.

We know that heresies of the kind were rampant in Padua. Tifi Odasi described in his *Macharonea* the *secta macaronea*, ostensibly an eating club: but there is reason[1] to think that when Cosmico was accused at Mantua of

[1] F. Gabotto, *L'Astrologia nel Quattrocento in rapporto colla civiltà.*

Chapel of the Planets

sodomy in 1489, the real charge was directed against the one-time secret heretical and astrological practices of this club.

One sees that on the cosmological side, at any rate, 15th-century study of the stars was a kind of play that satisfied cultural requirements. Owing to their unconscious bias in favour of an aesthetic approach to life, those who dabbled in cosmogony were not slow to reduce pre-existent dogma to terms of their own more immediate passions: and, mixing together every kind of doctrine, they were not troubled, or even interested, by the resultant contradictions. Reading Pontano's astrological poems one does not gather that he believed, nor that he disbelieved, in what was for him, as for his contemporaries, a poetic subject to which anyone was at liberty to extend exciting practical applications. Similarly, astrological symbols were often the means of personal philosophies.

It was so at Rimini. There is no reason to think that Sigismondo, any more than Francesco Sforza, trusted prediction. Perhaps he consulted occasionally, just as he was ready to be shriven upon his death-bed. A poem dealing with the heavens was written at his court, but, on the whole, it is severely astronomical. Basinio's *Astronomicon* does not help us to understand the Tempio sculpture. Basinio, a familiar of Sigismondo's, was perhaps the best Latin poet of the century. Many others beside the present author must have opened the *Astronomicon* with profound expectation, only to find nothing that would suit. The work follows rather mechanically the model of Aratus, the Greek original of which had been discovered in 1438.[1] There is room, of course, for some adulation of Sigismondo in the person of the sun; and for a reference to the sack of Constantinople which had recently occurred;[2] but otherwise there is nothing to interest us. Had Sigismondo cared much for prediction the *Astronomicon* would surely have revealed it. On the other hand, no poem was likely to reveal the deeper emotions of that age. One soon learns that rhetoric, and even poetry, were but the polite music of this intense age, and that the personal cult achieves projection foremost in visual art.

However, the *Urania* of Pontano, favourite at Naples, is an exception. This beautiful poem is not only avowedly astrological, but indeed throws some light on the planet sculptures at Rimini. No influence of the poem upon the sculpture is implied. It is conceivable, though, that the reliefs suggested some of the imagery and some of the myths of the poem. The earliest version of the *Urania* known to us is dated 1475. The planet sculpture was probably completed in 1457 or so. It is certain that Pontano was writing astrological poems as early as 1456, and since his home was in Umbria, it is possible that as a young man he was induced to see the new reliefs at Rimini.

At any rate there exists a community of feeling betwixt the *Urania* and the Tempio sculpture, the two foremost astrological expressions of the 15th century: and so

[1] See *La poesia astrologica nel Quattrocento*. Benedetto Soldati, Florence, 1906.

[2] *Astron.*, II, 457-487. Basinio calls for a crusade against the Turks.

we cannot do better than study some aspects of Pontano's poem.

He starts, as was usual, with an account of the moon, the luminary nearest the earth but also the prime symbol of magnetism or Influence. He thus sets the stage for the more distant planets and for the more complicated emotional projections that they represent; just as in the Tempio it is Diana with her moon that we first see up the aisle, suggesting to us all the powers and all the heavens.[1]

The second book contains a mixture of Platonic and Christian myths. At Naples, as at Rimini, neo-Platonism was the vogue. The intensified study of Plato, generally in neo-Platonic guise, was the current symbol of intellectual release: into the neo-Platonic language many personal and esoteric doctrines were translated. Sigismondo belonged to the vanguard of the movement: the fact that he brought from Greece the bones of Gemisthon Plethon to bury them in a Tempio sarcophagus leads one to suppose that he followed the neo-Platonic thought of this most remarkable man who found Italy ignorant and who returned to his native Sparta to renew its ancient constitution. Aristotle was out of fashion in the early Renaissance: owing to Averroistic and Scholastic associations there was attached to his name almost the stigma of the non-classical. Neo-Platonism was the new study: yet Aristotle's theory of motion was still a habit of mind: indeed, Aristotle was certain to come into his own again. The Aristotelian

[1] For an account of other means by which particular attention is called to the Diana relief, see p. 163.

Chapel of the Planets

non ante o post res sed in rebus idea of God really suited the
15th-century astrologers far better than the Platonic conceptions of which they were proud.

In the second book of the *Urania*, then, we are treated
to an account of the Platonic law of the Analogy. Earth
is the solid element that makes matter touchable: fire is
the mobile element that makes matter visible: the two
are united by air and water. God promulgates the law
to the assembled planets.[1] On his right Wisdom sits,
otherwise Jesus Christ; on his left Love, otherwise the
Holy Spirit. God tells the planets that with their Influences they must carve the world so that it shall correspond with his manufacture of the stars. Thus the planets
do not make the world, but they determine the mode of
its life.

The first book has described the character of each
planet's influence. Some of these characters are far more
clear than others. The conception of Jupiter is by no
means clear: he embodies Reason, yet at the same time
he is not unlike Jehovah the overpowering. The Sun
also is a prolific force whose many attributes leave with
the reader no very definite impression. The powers of
Jupiter, the Sun and Venus tend to overlap: but, otherwise, Venus is a clear positive force: the unmitigated
evil of Saturn is clear, the frightfulness of Mars, and
Mercury's power of accentuation. The astrological Mercury is always the final leaven, making good better and
evil worse, though providing also unexpected twists.
Like the moon, he is an embodiment of highly charged
currents and he reduplicates the mesh of the wires.

[1] In the *Timæus* the Demiurge holds a similar meeting.

Chapel of the Planets

Mercury symbolizes the essential ambivalence in all emotion: he, the messenger of the gods, is present at every turn. Nor are the other planets primarily moral forces. They are not so much good and bad principles as symbols of life and death. The pagan myths surrounding the names, with their bias in favour of unmorality, are here enforced. Reading Pontano, one realizes that he projected into the character of the planets the profound unfrightened philosophy of positive and negative forces, of the love instincts that mean life and of the destructive instincts that mean death. Into a pagan-Christian astrological hierarchy of Influences he has projected the forces controlling all men: the drama of the heaven's interactions are almost overtly the drama of his own unconscious life.

A similar projection in sculpture was, I feel, imbued almost consciously with personal reference at the Tempio. A familiarity with the reliefs brings the thought that the Isotta figure was Sigismondo's life-long influence, as intense a symbol as was ever devised of life, of renovation, of love; that it was with all the force of constant reaction from the fiercest hate that Sigismondo found himself subject to Isotta's calm and radiating magic. Sigismondo uses his omnipotence to exalt her to the status of non-moral powers. Isotta is Diana, is Mercury, is Venus, one above the other in the Tempio (Pl. 24). The personality of Sigismondo, I feel, was the actual means by which Agostino could express so uniquely the accumulated fantasies of stone and water and of the planets; or rather, Sigismondo's love for Isotta whose tomb he placed in the Tempio during her life and his, was the actual means. Agostino's stone forms, luminous and swimming on the stone[1], reduplicate Isotta's magnetism to which Sigismondo was, or wished to think he was, subject. Like the planetary orbits, her powers exercised him. She was the huntress Moon: and as the fruit of the waters is concreted into marble, so he would possess her clear magnetic charms stabilized in figures upon the stone. He needed these emblems and this shrine, perhaps because he sought and could not find a guiding star or a love worthy of his histrionic sense and of his ancestors; or more probably, in part because of this, and, in part, because he truly loved Isotta and felt the goddess in her. At any rate the Tempio sculpture magnifies the bond between them, a vaunted shield to stop the outside world as well as a mark to provoke its ugly religious horror.

I do not suggest that the reliefs embody more than the elements of this personal mythology. Details may correspond; and certainly the symbols of Sigismondo and Isotta fill every available space. On the other hand, the subjects represented, such as the planets and the sciences and the prophets and the putti, were current themes. The quality of Influence that Agostino's sculpture expresses is more pervasive than precise: we needed primarily to approach it from the side of stone and water and pure carving values, rather than in terms of

[1] It is perhaps significant that the high relief of the first chapels was not pursued further. Did the conception inspiring the Tempio become more clear as the work proceeded, and was it then that Agostino's luminous low-relief forms were evolved? It is probable that the low-relief figures on the walls of the first chapel on the right belong to this later period.

Chapel of the Planets

Sigismondo and Isotta. Still, since one feels at every turn that a personal myth inspires the Tempio, one is bound to take up any possible reference to Isotta. For instance, one notices that both Diana and Mercury in particular (Pls. 44, 45) (and Mercury's sex is glossed over) have the entranced, rather pig-like features which the medals of Pisanello and Matteo de' Pasti, the only authentic representations, suggest for Isotta: one cannot be certain, because the face on these medals is in profile. These pig-like features are common to many of the Tempio reliefs (Pls. 18, 29, 30, 43-47): and if we consider how that Sigismondo's poets introduced the person of Isotta (idealized in their verses, however, beyond the point which could have enlightened us) on every possible occasion, it does not seem unlikely that the court sculptor, working in what was, at that time, the more virile art, reproduced those features without excessive idealization throughout the series of reliefs, from habit if for no other reason: and no doubt the spell of Isotta rested upon Agostino too, so that he identified himself with his master.[1]

[1] I would have the reader understand that I am not the first person to find esoteric significance in the Tempio reliefs (though I have no acknowledgments to make to any previous interpretation). Hardly one investigator has resisted altogether some reference of the kind: I say 'resisted' because modern critics are rather shame-faced about it. Perhaps that is as well when one considers the effort of the late Dottore Giuseppe del Piano (*L'enigma filosofico del Tempio Malatestiano*. Forli, 1928), a local worthy who harboured a bee of some dimensions in his bonnet. Reading the signs of the Zodiac backwards, he found that the Tempio reliefs were a mystical interpretation of all religions, figuring the conclusive triumph of Christianity.

Another kind of excess (or infuriation) to which these pregnant

Chapel of the Planets

Again, one feels that the luminous, phosphorescent, lunatic figure of Mercury demands a wealth of comment (Pl. 45). What inspired so bucolic yet so exotic a form? Part of his vagueness answers to the Ptolemaic conception of Mercury whose sex, like his influences, is accounted variable. In the *Urania*, also, Mercury is described as so beautiful that one would have said he was the Virgin in whose zodiacal house he dwells, so brisk that one would have thought he would be transformed into one of Leda's swans. There is nothing brisk, it is true, about the Tempio Mercury. But the sex in a shape so luminous appears, none the less, most variable: this same lethargic, equivocal, fire, not so much a sexlessness as a bisexuality, informs several other planets, and the figures of many other reliefs besides. Was Yriarte right when he accounted the figure of St. Michael in the chapel with Isotta's tomb to be Isotta in the warrior's harness? Again, we must conclude that whatever the precise content may be, Sigismondo's erotic fantasies and exploits dictated a good deal of Agostino's style, a style which remained with him at Perugia. Influence, attraction, seduction, the intercourse of stone

yet baffling sculptures have given rise, was Yriarte's Greek theory, for some time generally accepted. Yriarte's idea was suggested by the Cufic script that appears on garment borders in some of the Arts and Sciences reliefs—*Rhetoric* and *Music*, for example. Now, these Cufic or Arabic letters were a common enough decorative motif in 15th-century art, and it is improbable that those used in the Tempio need any explanation or interpretation. But the presupposition always is that everything in the Tempio needs an explanation, and an exciting one at that. Giorgi and Amati had thought that the script was Greek: thereupon Yriarte concluded that these reliefs were ancient Greek reliefs brought by Sigismondo from the Morea.

Plate 45. Mercury.

Plate 46. Aquarius or Ganymede.

and water, are undoubtedly expressed by these reliefs: but it is impossible to define simply their erotic aim. On the whole, one would say that an expression so profound and fanciful is more likely to correspond with a few specific suggestions that summed up in Agostino's mind the atmosphere and the circumstances of the Riminese court, with a few dominant impressions rather than with some precise or elaborate programme. Agostino put the deepest Mediterranean fantasies of stone and water at the service of Sigismondo and his love: thus two spheres of fantasy were identified, in the case of the planet reliefs, exalted to the full by a further identification with astrological figures. The idea of Influence and attraction, the idea of Isotta's pervasive magic, stimulated in the sculptor the fantasies that his art inherited of fecund moisture in stone, of glimmering forms seen under water, of suctional forces congealed as shapes on the surface of the marble.[1]

[1]Shortly before going to press, I rediscovered in a 15th-century book a possible confirmation of the view I take of the Tempio sculpture's esoteric meaning, a view which, with a little further historical confirmation such as this may be, I would have announced in more definite (but possibly less accurate) terms. I do not myself consider it a matter of any importance for interpretation, to decide what were the exact *conscious* aims of the Tempio sculpture: but those who would always reject the evidence of the reliefs themselves in favour of some ghastly piece of historical testimony may be able to amuse themselves with the Latin passage below. It is from the last section (lib. 12) of Valturio's *De re militari* (British Museum 1483 copy). The sentences in question follow and are followed by many conventional compliments paid to Sigismondo as patron of the arts and as donor of sacred objects to the Tempio. Of the marbles in the interior Valturio writes: *Quibus vestiuntur pulcherrime sculptae inspiciuntur: unaque sanctorum patrum virtutem quattuor ac coelestis zodiaci signorum errantiumque siderum: sibillarum deinde musarumque et aliarum permultarum nobilium rerum imagines quae nec dum*

Chapel of the Planets

Each planet relief has the two zodiacal signs associated with it, one on either side, while the Moon or Diana has her one sign, the Crab, and the Sun or Apollo, here represented on the keystone of the arch, has the Lion. Diana, however, is provided with a second attendant, a youth riding a boat amid the spring tide (Pl. 48). To the twelve signs of the Zodiac, astrology attributes many meanings, even apart from the sun and the moon and the planets that pass through them. Thus, each sign represents roughly a month of the year: in the *Urania* Pontano works out twelve ages of the world to correspond with the twelve signs.

praeclaro lapicidae ac sculptoris artificio; sed etiam cognitione formarum liniamentis abste acutissimo et fine ulla dubitatio ne clarissimo hujus saeculi principe ex abditis philosophiae penetralibus sumptis intuentes litterarum peritos et a vulgi fere peritus alienos maxime possint allicere. The sibyls, muses and planets, says Valturio (addressing Sigismondo) are not only lovely as a result of the work the sculptors have put into them, but also because out of the store of your researches into the depths of philosophy (neo-Platonism) you yourself provided the shapes and features of these figures, bestowing them with such meaning that they *attract* to the utmost those cultured men who are far removed from the vulgar rabble. In other words (perhaps): Those in the know see these things with more instructed eyes than those of the vulgar rabble from whom, as from the Pope, the real intention of this sculpture must be concealed, and for whose benefit I now praise you in the most conventional fashion.

In attributing the scheme of the sculpture to Sigismondo's researches in philosophy, is the precise mention of features (*liniamentis*) a reference to Isotta, to whom so many of the reliefs may have borne some likeness, one that was not too obvious and therefore dangerous?

I am particularly struck by Valturio's use of the word *allicere*, 'to attract'. For it is an unusual word, and the first reference the dictionary gives for it is in connection with the loadstone: *Si magnetium lapidem dicam, qui ferrum ad se adliciat et attrahat* (Cic. *Div.*, I, 39, 86). So this word exactly expresses the magnetic quality that I attribute to the reliefs and which, as I think, they were intended to suggest.

Chapel of the Planets

Diana's sign, the Crab, is represented as hanging over Rimini (Pl. 14), provoking again the thought that in these representations the influence of the moon is exalted and equated with Isotta as the guiding star: though anyone who has bathed at Rimini will recognize that this is not in any case an inappropriate sign to hang over the town. It is, perhaps, worth repeating the new fable that Pontano gives for the Crab: for his is not a variation of the usual myth about the crab that pinched Hercules in the Lernian marsh. Pontano relates that Proteus, grand seducer of nymphs, has a new plot. Changing himself into a crab, he penetrates into the company of Naiads: he manages to make a conquest. Elated by his success, one day on the banks of the Eurotas he tries Diana, who has descended to bathe after the hunt. The prompt goddess changes herself into her planet, tearing into the sky with her assailant. Apollo, disgusted by the offence to his sister, passes every year over the miscreant's body, burning him with his flames (the heats of July). Jupiter, not to be left behind, puts a dishonourable mark on the back of the beast (two constellations in Cancer) and permits men to squander the Protean kingdom (summer navigation).

I shall not give the myths for the other signs of the Zodiac or describe what are the probable pagan figures associated with them in the Tempio series, except to say that Aquarius (Pl. 46) is doubtless Ganymede.[1] Aquarius

[1] Ricci, *op. cit.*, identifies this figure with Deucalion, on insufficient evidence, I think. Altogether, Ricci is not very reliable on the planet reliefs. Thus, his remarking that the hind legs of Taurus the Bull have probably been broken off shows, perhaps, that he is unaware that Taurus is generally represented as truncated. Again,

is the night house of Saturn: in astrology not Jove, but the older Italian god, Saturn, is implicated with Ganymede.[1] Saturn (Pl. 15) is represented in orthodox guise as an old man who devours his children as soon as they are born. None the less, Ganymede has the Isotta features: though he hurls the storms of winter he is young and beautiful, is Ganymede in fact who but pours out wine for the gods. Again one is aware of a heightened erotic symbolism that reinforces the direct and primary sexual symbolism of the old astrological myths. No matter the storms of winter: Isotta, young and serene, presides throughout the skies' hemispheres and interminable alternations. She gleams on high under Saturn as under Venus. She is Ganymede, she is Mercury, but above all she is the Moon, Diana who confounds the heights with the depths, goddess of waters, of pools and stones.

Ricci finds the full udders of Capricorn (Pl. 5) to be an anomaly. In Ptolemaic astrology, however, Capricorn is always accounted feminine.

[1] Cf.

> Saturno sodomita sen va a pede
> Trent' anni in torno, per venire un tracto
> A bever de la man di Ganymede.

Antonio Cornazzano, *De excellentium virorum principibus*. Dedicated to Borso D'Este. *Codice sessoriano*, 413. Bibl. Vitt. Emm. Rome.

Chapter Seven

The Final Picture

Behold an aerolith! Out of the blue, stone has poured in torrents over the blunt Gothic pins and needles, flooding with crystallizing foam the grey Germanic flanks.[1] It was not the first time that it rained building. In 1291 Palestine was the aerodrome, and upon a Syrian carpet the house of the Blessed Virgin[2] rose over the dead sea, landing at Tersalto near Fiume. In 1295 the Casa Santa took to the air again, this time by night. A landing was made near Recanati in a laurel grove. The miracle was recognized immediately, the laurels cleared, and the shrines of Loreto crept near the wooden, holy house.

Syria seated on a foothill of the Apennines was no stranger. For many centuries now the skinny datestone shot from its dry, sweet-wood covering, had overruled the smooth, green olives, tender with down, firm with moulding. What is the voice that cries in the wilderness when heard overseas among the succulent green and the

[1] This refers to Alberti's stone encasement of Gothic San Francesco.

[2] This is the legend as to how the Casa Santa found its way to Loreto, south of Ancona, subsequently chief centre of pilgrimage in Italy.

247

shadows? How sound the words of Paul of Tarsus among the willows and dykes? Far from desert and arid dates, far from the bazaars, those wells of whiteness like the lotus-flute bell of the leper sleeping in a sun-girt shade, far from the twilight walls, different levels, walls made for leaning and stations for attention to Solomon's ducts, water trickling under the dust, far from the dry months and the moon-cedars of Lebanon, far from the sudden explosion of the seasons; in Europe sailing with full canvas of moisture, in Europe the voice croaking in the wilderness becomes the plaintive Gregorian chant, brown date and white lazar-houses become the grey smocks and the grey stone, the parables become monk-ish tales and palm-like Gothic piers, and vaults prolific as the mustard tree.

Whence came this other building, from whence fell this encasement that fits like a strong and knotted gauntlet? The dispersed laurels take their revenge: behold this other miracle! They have stirred the heart of stone, precious marbles that sheeted the walls of San Apollinare in Classe, Roman foundations, tombstones galore tired of their dead, and Istrian stone at Fano. These hearkened to the laurels: compounded, a body grew in the upper air, and when all was ready, invested San Francesco.

Contact with its holy places quickens Christendom: the same contact is now supplied by the highly coloured pictures in prayer-books. For all the ugly carpentry of the village church and the imminence of Sunday lunch, the morning service is like Jonah in the belly of the monster, parting a once pagan sea on a voyage to Perga in Pamphylia. The brass of Judaism lies heavy on a

The Final Picture

Greco-Roman world, compressing praetor and centurion into forms of grace. Ananias falls dead before the communion plate, Ruth bows her head among the alien corn. In a mirage city of cisterns, Hezekiah turns his ebony face to the wall and dies. "Separate me Paul and Barnabas." The reader of the second lesson is drawing water from a well with the pitcher of the Samaritan woman. The verger peers round the font with the movement of a blind man creeping with his sores and boils out of the furze to touch the hem of a garment or to see men as trees walking. The insatiable psalms make the shadows rage, while in the open, beyond church walls, sunlight, like the Hellenic, blazes silent and dead, now of the nether-world of week-days. The dank, vaulty smell of religious stone and Bible and Sunday cleanliness is the same that blew from the emptied sepulchre after Golgotha and the rent veils, when the great stone went rolling from its mouth and the Hebraic linen was found folded. Rank, it is indeed, this Protestant quickening of a whittled sanctity with the brass and anathema of the Nearer East.

Not so in a Catholic country. In the Middle Ages Rome still was breathing. Syrian odours were less powerful along the open cloisters and pantheistic colonnades. Incense had another tang, the burning damask of the Saracens. Contact through the Crusades with holy places enlivened the West. The brightest steel of Turkish enterprise in a country where the Christian mind would be most receptive, kindled intelligence. Back in Europe, the universities of Paris, Padua and Bologna burst into new flame; and Vacarius chooses Oxford.

The Final Picture

And, even now at Rimini, even as the glorious, brightest sun dispersing dark, Phoebus of earliest day rises from the Adriatic, straight like the rush of the ringing diver from the deep when he lifts the lid of the jointed surface; as rays diffuse without betrayal of the strength of that progress, when eyes open to proud endeavour and to the sweet, near distances; even then too the air brings an odour from the Syrian land, faint this time, gracing the sunlight so that it be not hard. A new Turk[1] is among the holy places, Christian and Pagan. The cupolas of Byzantium, soft and ovular with a million lazy snippets of gold, yet flawless like eggshell, have begun to smoulder with volumes of foreboding. The barn-owl heads, thatched with bells and straw, those straight ones, the campanili of the lagoons, pick up the message from across the sea and give it to the kindred cupolas of Venice. Wood and stone communicate with gold, young marble springs up to watch. All building is alive with meaning. From Venice to Ravenna and on to Rimini, up from San Cyriaco at Ancona again to Rimini, swell voices of the Greco-Judaic world from the loaded little churches of Christendom, flawless and continuous like eggshells. Greco-Judaic! Not against the advancing Turk alone this whispering. After their long admixture, Greek is trying to disentangle himself and define the Jew. Revolt. The riderless and unridable horses of St. Mark's, disdainers of an incense-perfumed stable, metropolitan cavalry, have cleared a way for the piazza. Precious marbles that sheet the interior of San

[1] The Ottoman Turks, who in 1453, three years after Alberti had made his design for the Tempio encasement, and while building was in progress, took Byzantium.

The Final Picture

Apollinare in Classe have deserted in the night, a
hundred carts full. . . .

Not only because Rimini is on the sea, but also since,
as we have imagined, the air was humming with Venetian presage, did the Tempio shelter marine aspiration.
The Adriatic can be terrible at Rimini. In August 1442,
when Sigismondo and Sforza were pinned up in the
Marches, so horrible a storm broke over Rimini that the
inhabitants thought that the end of the world had come.
Many lost their lives, some killed by blocks of hail whose
like had never been seen. According to Clementini, a
tidal wave carried a ship in the harbour on to the roof
of a warehouse. Nonplussed by the silting Po, the Adriatic has retreated from Aemilia, vents her frustration
upon the Pentapolis coast. To curb their effrontery, to
patch up their hostility, to force them by interpene-
tration to serve the union of the elephant and the rose,[1]
an influence over sea and land must be invoked so powerful in transfusion, that there comes to be but one essence
of which previously elemental natures are the stuff,
their peculiarities the adornment. Such power has the
pale moon, Diana, queen both of the pool and of the
thicket, goddess of the chase and of fish, of sea and of the
mountains. For with her wand of twanging light she
impels transfusion out of air and earth and water, out of
fire too, out of the sun. So, in the likeness of the influxion
caused by Diana, effluence of elephant nature, effluence
of rose nature are miraculously induced and sustained.

One *feels* this mythology in the Tempio. Diana ap-

[1] The respective symbols of Sigismondo and of Isotta and of their
love.

The Final Picture

pears only once, in company with the planets: but, whatever his subject, the execution of Agostino, even when serving the purposes of Pasti, betrays this mythology inspired by Sigismondo. Further, in a sense, Isotta herself is Diana, because she is mistress of the moon-influence to which she is also subject, because the power, the magic she exerts over Sigismondo is, like all female seductiveness, magnetic, a form of indiscriminate suction drawing in diverse material, that, too, most foreign to movement.

The sun, of course, could not do it. Isotta as the sun could not do it, although with her power she could dry up Sigismondo's evil humours as they formed, she could bring promise to the surface. But what of the deepest sea?—all is darkness. What of the endless depth of Sigismondo's soul, not the showing of it? The rose cannot be stamped on such formlessness. What of the storm clouds that put out the sun, what of the floods and broken crops, what of the sea's feud with the stampeding mountains? So huge the gusto, a power of darkness is invoked that by dizzy influence, distinctness and command may yet penetrate the roots. Sigismondo and Isotta, mountain and sea, rose and elephant, sun and storm, only by this magic can they meet in entirety, all outward, at the norm of human expression. But, mark you, if it is in the dimness of the night that these miracles befall, yet each object is still distinct, is but transformed, not obscured by the magic[1] dark: so we may see the

[1] Hereon to the end, the reader is referred to all my illustrations of the Tempio, particularly the planet reliefs, the Crab, and, above all, the influxion of the moon relief (Pl. 48).

The Final Picture

transformation ourselves. Moreover, it is not a neutral stuff that the moon conceives from elemental natures. Diana, too, is under orders from Sigismondo. Fusion of panorama with sea, elephant with rose, results in an army of music, children in a silver paradise riding leviathans, hurling the fiery stars, playing with left-over scraps of the old elements, imprisoning air in trumpets, using the trick of water as fancy dresses, thumping hard upon clumps of earth, as upon cymbals.

And not inappropriate, when in 1461, Sigismondo near ruin, without money, the old roof of the aisle rotting, the new chapels without a covering and without the prospect of one, not inappropriate was the rain that drenched the marble sculptures. For in unplumbed depths Agostino had bought his stone: his draperies open and close like the rhythmic washing to and fro of tresses of seaweed clothing a far rock beneath clear water, moving even when the surface is unruffled; and like such a rock the heads of the putti are polished by the invisible weight, the listless movement of the water. But the depth is dark; yet there is whiteness only here at the bottom where nothing is still. This court of dolphins, maidens and infants, unsuppressed by centuries of watery weight, have broken through the ocean, have dried themselves by penetration of the marble, and now fill hoarse unaccustomed lungs with breeze. Scales fall from their eyes. They have been drawn up by a spring tide, by the curious influence of Diana, who keeps them swaying as if the palpitating waters still rocked their hair. Water spirit, young Aquarius, minion of Saturn, at the beck of Diana is invading the land. Meanwhile an alliance has been negotiated with Auster, and a soft south wind and water and air, under the aegis of Diana, dissolve inflexible roots, forcing by dilution admixture which normally would take a myriad years. On an island of jungle land surrounded by the dolphin-populated flux, the elephant and the lion have walked down to join the inspired flood and to vouchsafe the secret places of the wood. Mountains jump up in mid-ocean, scattering the sea. Now Diana re-enters her pagan grave and submits to being resurrected as the sods are upturned by the process she has set in motion. Her place in the sky is taken by the Crab who has stolen up out of the Adriatic over Rimini. Due to the ineluct-able union of water and air, under the aegis of Diana, natural forces are suspended, in the flood of moonlight trees may root in the sea, dolphins sport the land, and ships brush their rigging against the fortress, moonlight twanging at the spars. Now Diana has mounted her chariot, and as she climbs the sky to displace the Crab, fish slip off the board, their metallic bodies strike the moonlight. For all is molten silver, and up from the earth comes a bucolic Mercury, his sodden garment limp and worn by the grave to single threads. Immed-iately he assumes his position, one foot on land, one in water, and to give the effect of continuity, as if no inter-ruption had occurred, he has gathered the cock of vigilance to him, also several spirits of the dead; and now he ties on his winged sandals and fixes a cloud to his knee as if he had this moment (forgetting the spirits of the dead) rushed down from Olympus. The influence at

Plate 47. The Twins.

Plate 48. Influxion caused by the moon.

The Final Picture

work sets the lute he carries a-whirring, and two serpents hasten to join his caduceus.

Diana is at her height. Sea and sea-life mount the shore still higher without harm to the land because of the infusion of air and moonlight in the heavy water. The mysteries of ocean and of earth, taut now and exemplified to the last atom, at peace, together they are forging the new element which shall the better sustain the offspring of dust and water, the living form, their offspring of a now-remembered marriage before the feud. Entranced human forms flash up, their sex alone indistinct as with the alert and hypnotised Mercury, as with Jupiter. Here are the Twins, hand in hand: their young bodies glisten beneath the filmy draperies that guard their breasts like administering clouds that hasten to tend the moon, to hide her tired eyes some night when her laborious tears of cold silver shall not fall into gravity; and thus she cannot set influence to work as now she does. Indeed, Diana is at her height, and in an excess of hypnotic power she summons the yet remaining lords of the universe. Saturn comes in haste, his beard unkempt, a Phrygian night-cap upon his head. But Mars has never unhammered his armour since the ancient times, his chariot is ready, and it needed but one word from him to set the wolf baying at his horses' feet. They hasten to enrich the element that sustains the human form to its greatest glory. The mountains rise and drop in the even, chorded light, a god in ecstasy on every peak as, breaking the leaf of tuneful silver, Venus comes reborn out of the further sea into the new element, her chariot drawn this time by two white swans. Trees stand upon the tallest waves that move in procession behind her. Doves descend to give her greeting and to inspect the open shell, her birthplace, that she flourishes. As she touches land she disappears. Infusion is complete. Nothing remains to the outer senses, all is music now, imperceptible to the ear, loud in the blood.

Index

Index

Index

Index

Index

Index

Pius II, Pope, 198, 199 n., 234.
Planets, the, 214, 216, 234, 238, 252-256.
Plaster, 38.
Plastik, 108, 131.
Plato, 62, 210, 218, 222.
— of Tivoli, 228.
Platonic law of the Analogy, 238.
Pompeii, 93.
Pontano, 235, 244, 245.
— his philosophy, 239.
Poros stone, 57.
Portland stone, 51 n., 53.
— — basebed, 50.
— — whitbed, 50.
Poseidon, 92.
Posidonius, 221.
Pound, Ezra, 26, 230 n.
Ptolemy, 228.
Pugin, 46.
Pyramids, the, 51.

Q

Quattro Cento, 25, 41, 55, 97, 98, 117, 125, 128, 132, 151, 152, 153, 157, 158, 161, 192, 196, 205, 208, 223, 224, 225, 228.
— — definition of, 25.
— — design, 179, 180, 189 n., 192.
— — relief, definition of, 153.
see also Fantasies of stone and water.
Quito, 32.

R

Rain, 37, 79, 80; *see also* Water.
Rain-gods, 79-89.
Ravenna, 176, 181, 208 n.
— Baptistry of the Orthodox, 129.

Ravenna, San Appollinare in Classe, 189 n., 248, 251.
— — — Nuovo, 129.
Recanati, 247.
Relief carving, 105, 106, 114, 116, 117, 118, 126-129, 135, 149-163.
Rembrandt, 120.
Renaissance, the, 98, 99, 117, 125, 202, 231.
Renoir, 137.
Rhythm and Space, 141, 144.
Ricci, Corrado, 194 n., 245 n.
Rimini, 156, 169-176, 245, 250, 251.
— history of, 172, 173.
see also Tempio Malatestiano, Malatesta, Sigismondo.
Rocks, distribution of, 37 n.
Rodin, 120.
Romagna, 177.
Romanesque reliefs, 128.
Romantic poets as belonging to the Industrial Age, 220.
Rome, 70, 72, 83, 84, 124, 206, 207, 217, 221, 249.
See also Travertine.
Rose, *see* Malatesta Emblems.
Rossellinos, the, 133.
Rubbed forms, 112, 113.
Rubens, 121.
Rubicon, the, 169.

S

Salamis, 68, 69.
Sandstone, Indian, 28.
Sandstones, 49, 50.
— light of, 54, 55.
Sargon, King, 61.
Saturn, 246.
— relief of, 156, 246.
Sedimentary rocks, 30; *see also* Limestone, Sandstones, Clayey stones.

262

Index

Index